IMAGES
of America

EAST SACRAMENTO

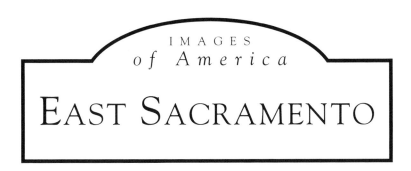

IMAGES
of America

EAST SACRAMENTO

Edited by Lee M.A. Simpson

ARCADIA

Published by Arcadia Publishing
Charleston SC, Chicago IL, Portsmouth NH, San Francisco CA

Printed in Great Britain

Library of Congress Catalog Card Number: 2004109466

For all general information contact Arcadia Publishing at:
Telephone 843-853-2070
Fax 843-853-0044
E-mail sales@arcadiapublishing.com
For customer service and orders:
Toll-Free 1-888-313-2665

Visit us on the internet at http://www.arcadiapublishing.com

CONTENTS

ACKNOWLEDGMENTS

This project is the result of a unique collaborative effort between the history department at California State University, Sacramento, and the Sacramento Archives and Museum Collection Center (SAMCC). The book is the culmination of a semester-long research project conducted by students in a senior research seminar. The staff at SAMCC graciously opened their collections to us in exchange for receiving all royalties from the sale of this book. Unless otherwise noted, all of the photographs in this collection come from SAMCC. Special thanks are due to staff members Pat Johnson, Sally Stephenson, and James Henley, who patiently answered student questions and tirelessly hunted down missing photographs, and to SAMCC volunteer Birdie Boyles, who provided significant information on Barbara Worth Oakford.

In addition to the staff and volunteers at SAMCC, several East Sacramento residents, including Cindy Woodward, Carol Roland, Erwin and Carol Shaltes, Marilyn Meister Hanson, Kerry Phillips, Sue Millward-Ferguson, and Steven Ballew, opened their family photo albums and shared memories of life in the community. Cindy Collins, who along with Kim Kuenlen designed a series of storyboards of East Sacramento history, provided additional information on this particular set of photos. Local churches helped flesh out the religious history of the community. Special thanks is due to Lee Ramsey of Faith United Methodist Church, John Ranlett of the Lutheran Church, members of Sacred Heart of Jesus Church, Barbara Gibson of the Mosaic Law Congregation, and Bishop Farrimond of the Church of Jesus Christ of Latter Day Saints. In addition, Rosemary Navarro provided photographs for Sutter Memorial Hospital.

The text of this book relies heavily on several published and unpublished research projects. The work of Steven Avella, Amanda Meeker, and Angel Tomes has helped us establish both the local historical context for the photographs and a broader national context.

INTRODUCTION

As designated by the City of Sacramento Planning and Building Department, East Sacramento is bounded on the North by the American River, on the East by Watt Avenue, on the South by the Light Rail right-of-way and Folsom Boulevard, and on the West by Alhambra Boulevard. This geographic designation, however, does not reflect the community's sense of place. For the purposes of this book, East Sacramento is instead designated by the American River to the North, Folsom Boulevard to the South, Alhambra Boulevard to the West, and California State University, Sacramento, and Elvas Avenue to the East. We have consciously chosen to exclude River Park from this book. Although the neighborhood is part of East Sacramento broadly defined, we felt it has a distinct enough feel to warrant a book of its own.

East Sacramento development began in the 1890s as a typical American streetcar suburb with the laying of steetcar lines by the Sacramento Electric Power and Light Company. By 1905 Sacramentans were building suburban houses in the area, although agriculture continued to dominate into the 1920s. Reflecting the vision of growth for the city, by 1908 the neighborhood's farmland had been fully platted for development and electric lines strung. This created the curiously incongruous spectacle of dairy farms and sheep ranches side by side with the homes of downtown merchants and other professionals. Indeed, the area's main developers, Charles Wright and Howard Kimbrough, sold their developments as a country oasis, "just a fifteen minute ride from downtown." East Sacramento became an integral part of the city in 1911 when it was annexed to the city.

East Sacramento's residential growth occurred at a time of transition for America's growing cities from streetcar suburbs to automobile suburbs. As early as 1914, Wright and Kimbrough offered homes that included garages, signifying their understanding that the automobile would replace the streetcar. Nonetheless, the J Street Streetcar line, extending from Twenty-eighth to Forty-sixth Streets, continued to provide the main mode of transportation to downtown into the 1940s, when the streetcars were replaced by automobiles and buses.

Despite East Sacramento's reputation as an exclusive neighborhood (the result of Wright & Kimbrough Tract 24—the Fabulous Forties), the community's many distinct neighborhoods reflect the true economic diversity of Sacramento's residents. Houses vary from the relatively modest units of the J Street Court (now Dolores Way), to the upscale, expensive units of McKinley Park and the Fabulous Forties. Residents also reflected some of the ethnic diversity of Sacramento. Families of Italian, German, English, and Irish descent could be found throughout the neighborhoods. Restrictive covenants on property deeds kept this a "white" neighborhood until the 1954 Supreme Court decision in *Shelley v. Kramer* declared race-based covenants unenforceable. Nonetheless, people of color could be found in the neighborhood working as domestics.

In the 1920s, East Sacramento became increasingly attractive to Sacramento's growing professional class. Numerous business and professional men relocated from the older areas of Sacramento to the more fashionable East Sacramento. A virtual merchants row developed on

Cutter (Thirty-ninth) and Maple Streets (Thirty-eighth), home to the auto and train manufacturers Charles and Albert Meister; S.J. Lubin, vice president of Weinstock & Lubin; Walter Rennie, secretary of Hall, Luhrs & Company; attorney J.W.S. Butler; and L.F. Breuner of Breuner Furniture. Despite their economic success, the homes they built were not mansions, but homes for growing upper-middle-class families. Although the Great Depression rocked real estate values and forced some of these professional families to leave the neighborhood, postwar growth reestablished the area as one of the most desirable in Sacramento.

Like the men of merchant's row, most residents of East Sacramento found employment downtown. Physicians, lawyers, and businessmen rode the streetcars to work alongside blue-collar workers such as railroad employees, janitors, truck farmers, and cigar salesmen. Some local employment did develop in the form of small businesses, many family-run, providing services to the area's residents. These businesses have, in some respects, provided the connecting skein of community. Stability is their hallmark. Many employees, whether sodajerks or barbers, spent their working lives in the same jobs. The People's Pharmacy run by the Bone family, Wambles at Forty-seventh and H, and Knott's Pharmacy became local gathering places where young people congregated after football games. The Bones were famous for giving away free milkshakes after wins.

Today East Sacramento is a vibrant community characterized by residential stability. Those who move to East Sacramento stay. Many homeowners are second- or third-generation Sacramentans and some homes are still owned by the same families that built them. A sense of pride in the community is evident in the care and upkeep of homes and businesses. There is an abiding sense of history in the community and a growing awareness of the contributions residents have made to their neighborhood and their city.

Over the decades, the character of East Sacramento has been maintained despite additions, remodels, scrape-offs, and infill. Many of the conveniences with which Charles E. Wright attracted buyers to Tract 24 in 1914 still attract residents today. The community is well planned, with shade trees, beautiful landscaping, paved streets, sidewalks, gas, electricity, sanitary sewers, and proximity to downtown. East Sacramento furnished needed space for a growing city and continues today as a distinctive neighborhood of character even though buyers are no longer attracted by the "low down payments." With the hard work of an emerging group of preservation-minded citizens, the area may yet be protected from incompatible development. Though unsuccessful in protecting the beautiful Alhambra Theater, torn down to make way for a Safeway Supermarket, citizens are now united to make sure such destruction never happens again.

In the following chapters, this book will examine the history of East Sacramento's neighborhoods from their earliest development to the present. It will explore the architectural diversity of the neighborhood, the families that made a life here, the impact of transportation and commercial developments, as well as the rich community feeling that followed the building of schools, churches, and recreational outlets.

One

FOUNDATIONS FOR THE FUTURE

By James W. Sharum

The development of East Sacramento did not happen overnight or in a strict linear progression. Despite a boom in construction and property sales during the ten years before and after the 1911 annexation of East Sacramento into Sacramento proper, by 1920 much of East Sacramento remained arable land. East Sacramento was not developed in a discernable pattern as a result of private land owners who sold parcels whenever it was deemed profitable. Real-estate developers kept an eager watch for available land to be subdivided and turned into luxurious yet affordable neighborhoods meant to draw both upper- and middle-class homeowners out of the city. Following the inception of the affordable automobile after 1908 with Henry Ford's Model T, American land became more accessible than it had ever been. With transportation consisting of more than electric streetcars, East Sacramento was able to develop away from the central lines laid down by the Pacific Gas and Electric Railway.

One of the most important developers to begin this process of subdivision was the team of Charles Wright and Howard Kimbrough. Wright and Kimbrough were responsible for some of the most well known developments in East Sacramento, such as the Fabulous Forties, and for the infrastructure around which much of East Sacramento developed. They designed neighborhoods with large tree-lined lots, wide streets, and amenities such as sanitary sewers and streetlights. They also strove for modernity by including garages on lots—thus acknowledging the trend that would become the norm within a few years. After realtors developed property in East Sacramento neighborhoods, they were able to sell them off at increasingly reasonable prices, allowing people of middle-class status to enter the neighborhood. Because lots did not have houses included on them, property owners in the developments could choose—provided they followed covenants set by the developers—who they wanted to have build their homes and how much they wanted to spend. This personal choice in builders gives East Sacramento an eclectic mix of architecture; however, the trend to use pre-designed pattern homes increased steadily through the middle of the 20th century. One of the most notable architectural teams in the East Sacramento area was the firm of Dean and Dean, responsible for some of the most elegant homes in East Sacramento.

The push to develop East Sacramento was not without its setbacks. Much of the East Sacramento land that abutted the American River was reclamation land that, because of its low-lying position, was prone to floods. Record floods in 1951, 1956, and 1964 prompted the city to take more aggressive measures to ensure that its levee system was strong enough to withstand severe flooding. These floods slowed some prospective residents from building until after California State University, Sacramento, and River Park became more established.

In addition to flooding slowing the process of suburbanization in East Sacramento, the Great Depression also contributed to a wane in building. Though much of East Sacramento had been filled in prior to 1920, especially in the Fabulous Forties, the Great Depression brought chaos to many who lived in East Sacramento and kept those who would have built there at bay. There were increases in property sales and foreclosures by people who had overextended themselves throughout East Sacramento. The area continued to grow, however, and retains much of the original attractiveness that developers once envisioned when platting the communities within its borders.

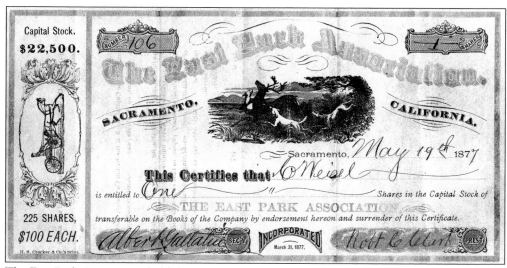

The East Park Association held the title to the land that became McKinley Park. Though they almost sold the property several times, McKinley Park became one of the more upscale East Sacramento neighborhoods in 1877.

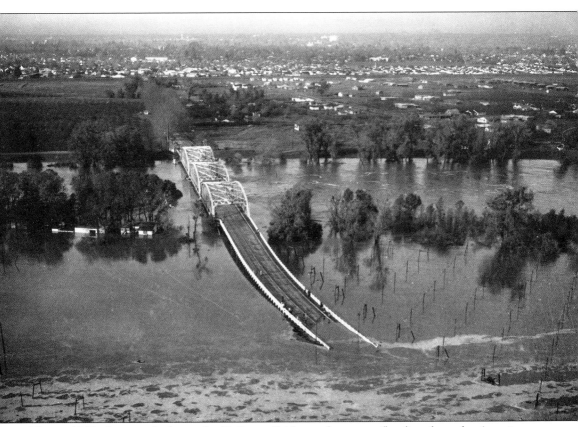

This *c.* 1930 photograph shows the H Street Bridge under severe flooding from the American river. Now known as the Fair Oaks Bridge, the area has been brought under control by levees and is now home to California State University, Sacramento.

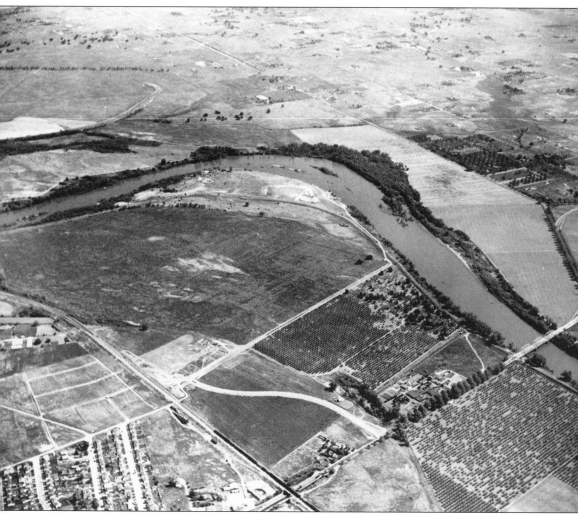

This *c.* 1930 aerial photograph shows a sparsely populated River Park. It is interesting to note the dominance of agricultural production still present along the American River at this time. Note also the wide berth given to the river for fear of flooding.

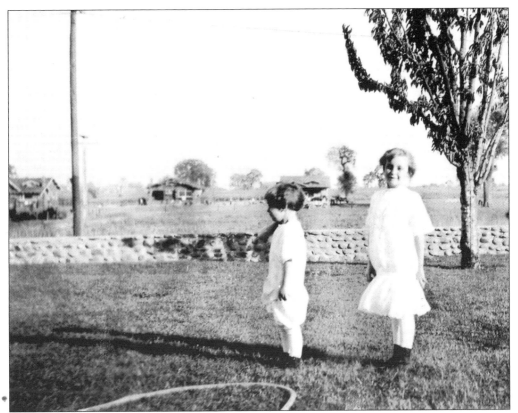

In this 1904 image, August and Dorothy Meister pose in the front yard of their home on Thirty-ninth Street. Note the farms in the background, indicating the agricultural roots of East Sacramento. (Photo courtesy Marilyn Meister Hanson, background enhancements courtesy Steven Ballew.)

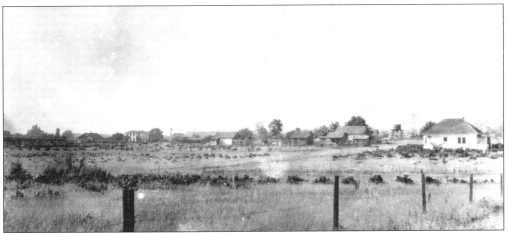

This 1910 photograph shows the Bullock home along with shacks owned by the Mellors, Jennings, and Woodhouses. The few houses and absence of platted streets show the contrast between private property and the developed communities that were to come. Private property was a major hurdle that developers such as Wright and Kimbrough had to overcome before suburbanization could occur.

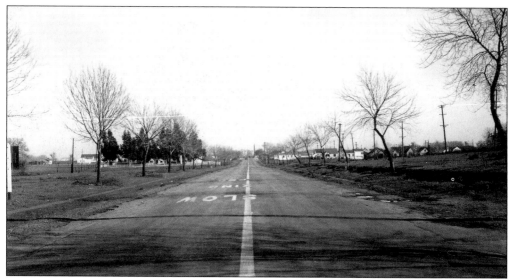

Taken in 1940, this street scene is a good example of both the open expanse still visible in pre–World War II East Sacramento and the care taken by the platters to create alluring, wide, tree-lined streets complete with power lines for expansion.

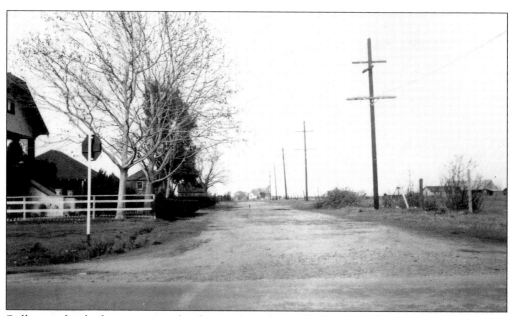

Still an unfinished community, the dirt roads in this c. 1940 picture show the transformations left to be made in East Sacramento. Note the architectural variety in the houses on the left.

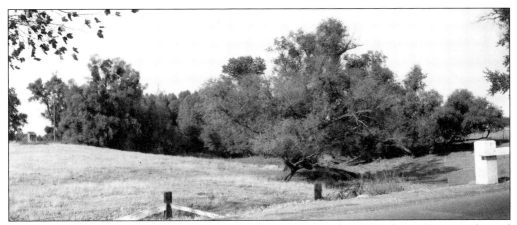

While Sacramento is still referred to as a city of trees, note in this 1939 photo the natural stand of large trees at Fifty-seventh and H Street, which are no longer in existence today. The removal of large stands of trees, such as this one, in favor of private homes shows the sacrifices made in order to allow for increases in suburbanized land.

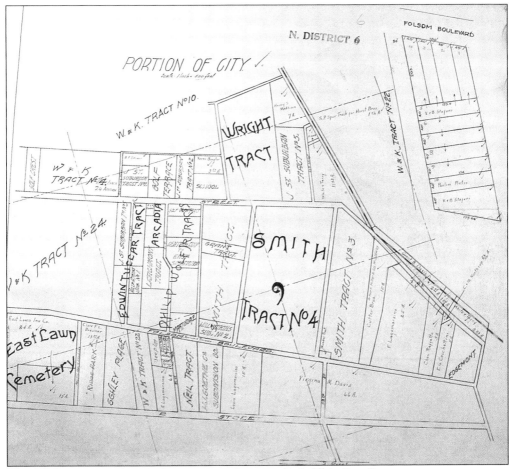

The 1925 tax assessor's map demonstrates the sporadic infill in East Sacramento.

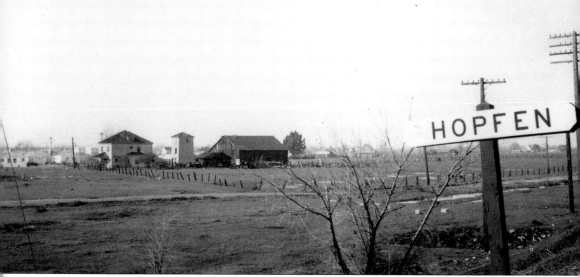

In this 1940 photo, hop fields along the H Street subway became the entrance to both California State University, Sacramento and River Park. Note the German sign showing some of the ethnic variety in the area.

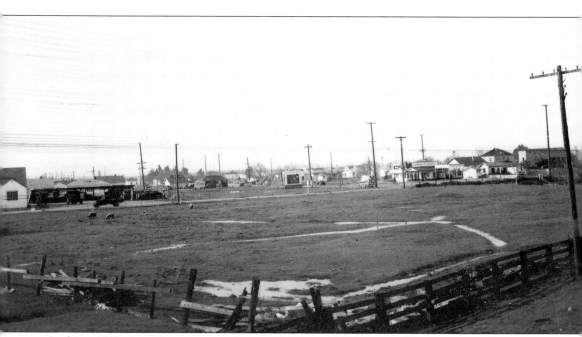

In this *c.* 1940 photo, houses encroaching on the Daniel McCarty ranch near H Street demonstrate the changing priorities of land use in East Sacramento from agricultural to residential.

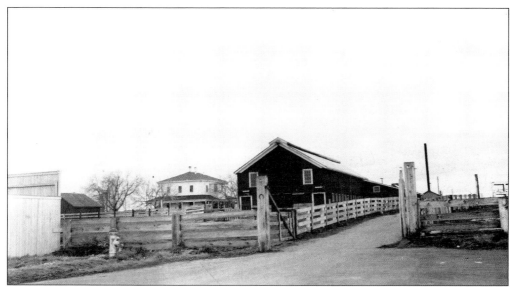

Erected in 1850, the Tivoli House at Thirty-first and B Street was later moved to 4590 C Street, the entrance to property bought by Wright and Kimbrough from the Meister family for $70,000. Formerly a dairy, it became an automobile accessible suburb with 100 homes at an average of $5,000 a home. This photo dates from *c.* 1941.

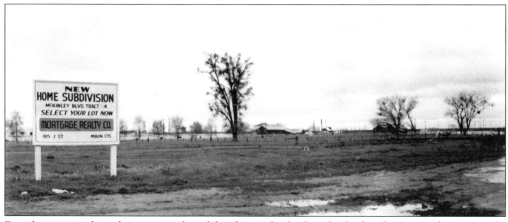

Developers purchased raw agricultural land on which they built developments from scratch. Wright estimated that 50 homes would be developed on the lot shown in this *c.* 1941 photo within a year, showing the strength of the market despite the effects of the Great Depression.

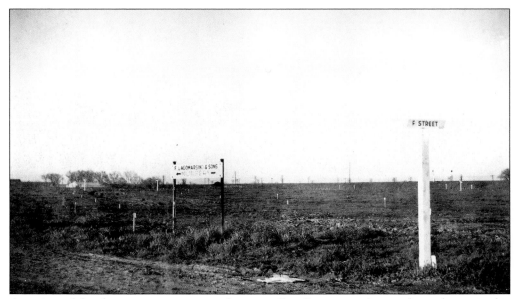

A variety of development companies took part in East Sacramento's growth, as shown in this c. 1946 photo. Lagomarsino and Sons purchased these lots at Forty-sixth and F Street. Development in East Sacramento was almost solely dependent on private land owners' desire or need to sell land off to developers who would offer them the best price.

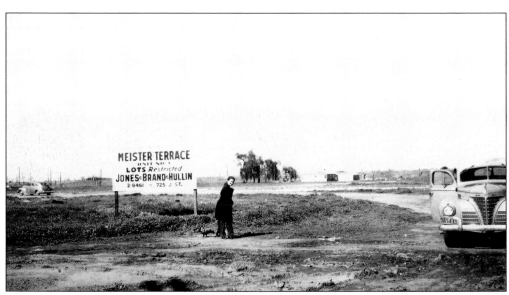

This property at Forty-first and A Street had been owned by the Meister family, who were some of the largest land owners in East Sacramento and kept much of their land near the river private through the 1940s. This photo dates from c. 1948.

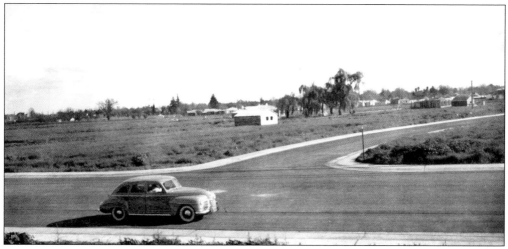

Taken in 1948, this photograph clearly shows the amount of infill left in the Elvas area. Growth had slowed after the Great Depression because of property foreclosures, but lots were still selling in this area for $1,050 and up.

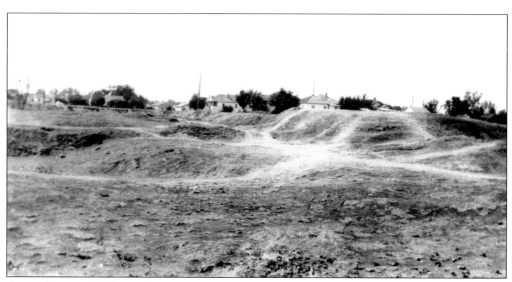

A gravel pit at Fifty-first and M Street was later turned into East Portal Park. In this c. 1945 photo, the houses over the ridge appear to be smaller than some of the homes typical of the Fabulous Forties denoting that this area may have been designated as more of a working-class neighborhood.

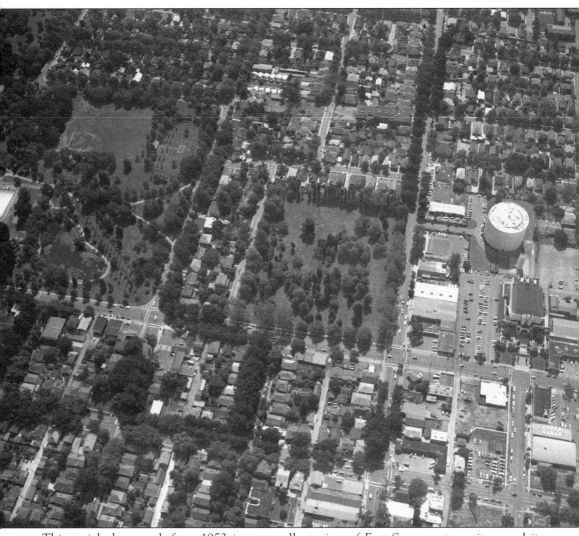

This aerial photograph from 1953 is an excellent view of East Sacramento as it neared its completion. The only visible chunk of open land eventually became Sutter Middle School.

Two

A 15-Minute Ride from Downtown

By Barbara Smith Eychaner

The flood plain of the American River provided East Sacramento, like the rest of the Central Valley of California, with good soil, ready access to water, and the relatively flat land that made it superb for farming, orchards, and dairies. So it is not surprising that many of the first dwellings in East Sacramento were farmhouses. Eventually it became more profitable to grow houses in this area so close to downtown. Folks such as the Inderkums, who had a dairy at Fortieth and J Streets, gradually sold off their land as farming became either less lucrative or simply too difficult. The last eight acres they sold became a development of 64 modest homes. Like the Inderkum home, some of the earliest houses in Sacramento were second-floor flood homes, built a full flight up to avoid the inevitable floods that came through the valley. After the levy was built and dams upstream on the American River reduced the chance of flooding, many of the second-floor houses added apartments or additional living space on the ground floor.

Among the families building homes in East Sacramento in the early 20th century were Louis and Clara Breuner, owners of the Breuner Furniture Company. Breuner's sold all the things families in East Sacramento wanted for their homes: straight-back wooden chairs and secretaries, three-piece parlor suites, kitchen tables with rat-proof flour bins, a kneading board, and a special drawer for the rolling pin. Wallpaper, oilcloth, window shades, and instructions for measuring wall-to-wall carpet were also available, as were bathroom fixtures and dress forms by 1914.

Adjacent to Cutter Street and just south of J Street from the Inderkums' property, Wright and Kimbrough developed Tract 24. In December 1914, *The Sacramento Bee* described the addition as homes "to enjoy life . . . be perfectly happy and contented." Houses were equipped with tile fireplaces, window seats, walnut woodwork, a built-in buffet in the dining room, wallpaper, lighting fixtures, complete cabinets in the kitchen, a screened porch, and space in the rear for a garage. And only $575 would seal the deal! As East Sacramento grew, many of the homes were built in the Craftsman style, first introduced in California about 1903, with low-pitched gabled roofs, wide eave overhangs, porches supported by columns, and exposed roof rafters. Then as now, a variety of other architectural styles contributed to the appeal of the community; no one style predominated and all seem to complement each other. All found a place in East Sacramento: steep-pitched roofs of Tudors, with front-facing gables and false-half timbering; colonial revivals with symmetrical facades, entryways supported by columns, windows with double-hung sashes;

Monterey revivals with distinctive cantilevered second-floor balconies and stucco exteriors; French eclectic with brick, stone, or stucco exterior wall treatments, flared eaves, and massive chimneys; Spanish eclectic, with low-pitched red tile roofs, arched doorways, and stucco exteriors; and Italian renaissance with tile roofs, arch doorways, large ornate first story windows, and decorative brackets supporting widely overhung eaves. Many of these are spectacular homes—such as the Pollock house on Forty-fifth Street that Gov. Ronald Reagan and his family rented in 1967 from city councilman and Mrs. Dain J. Domich.

Small developments such as the J Street Court were home during the 1930s to families who made their livelihood from working as telephone operators, carmen, or foremen for the Southern Pacific Railroad, bank tellers, bank examiners, salesmen, bakers, and superintendents of schools. The homes on J Street Court were very similar but varied in the detailing. There were also very modest homes, such as the four-room frame house built on Thirty-eighth Street by Ellen Boden in 1924 for $2,200. Jerry Galvin, a cook, and his wife, Esther, lived in that home for more than 30 years, from about 1949 into the 1980s, a testimony to the stability of the neighborhood.

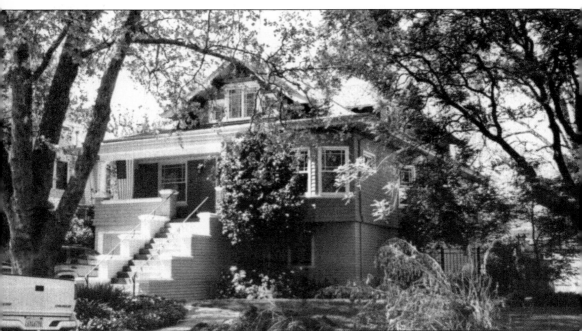

Raised above ground level, second-story flood homes like this one, shown in 2004 on Thirty-ninth Street, were typical of many in midtown Sacramento and of early homes in East Sacramento prior to construction of the levy and dams upstream along the American River. (Photo by Barbara Smith Eychaner.)

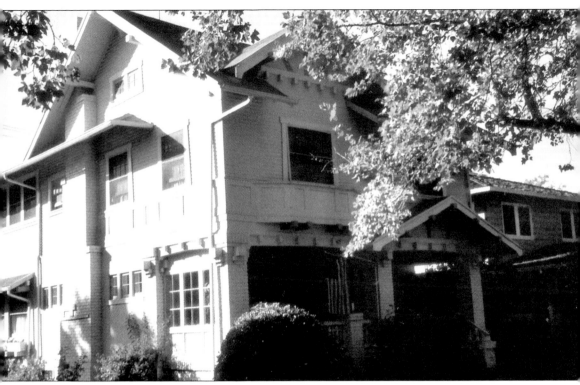

Both Charles Wright and Howard Kimbrough, East Sacramento developers, built their homes in the area. Wright's house, pictured here in 2003, was one of the first homes constructed in Tract 24. (Photo courtesy of Carson Hendricks.)

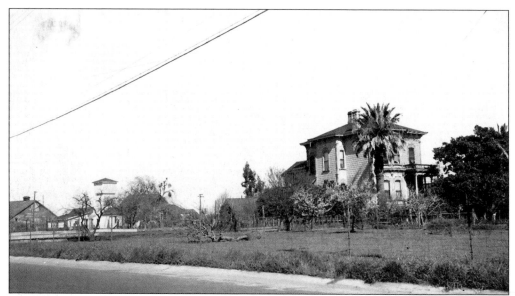

The sizable estate accumulated by George Terry and William W. White included ground that would later become California State University, Sacramento. At the time of Terry's death in 1943, the estate near the intersection of Fifty-ninth and J Streets included more than 500 acres valued at about $142,000. This photo was taken in 1941.

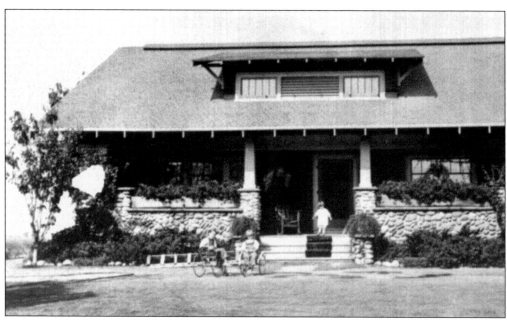

Built in 1905, just a block and a half from the streetcar line on J Street, the Albert Meister house, shown in this c. 1908 photo, remained in the family until 1977. The homes of Albert and his brother Charles, among the first on the eastern outskirts of Sacramento on Cutter Street (now Thirty-ninth Street), were separated by an orchard. (Photo courtesy Marilyn Meister Hanson.)

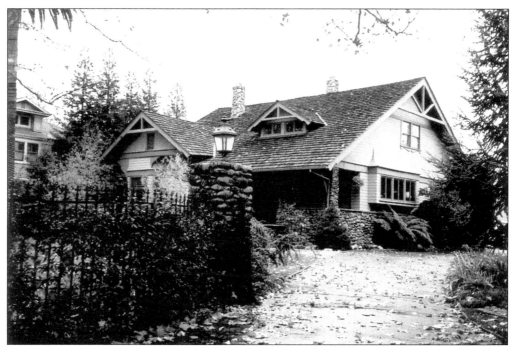

Charles and Edward Meister built homes in close proximity to their brother Albert. Charles's house, shown above in 2004, is the most ornate of the three. Edward's house, shown below in 2004, was located one block away on Thirty-eighth Street. (Photos by Carson Hendricks and Melissa Montag.)

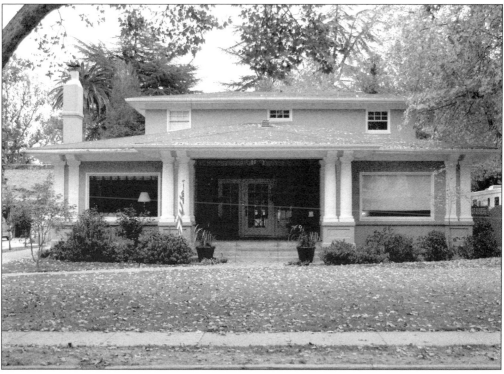

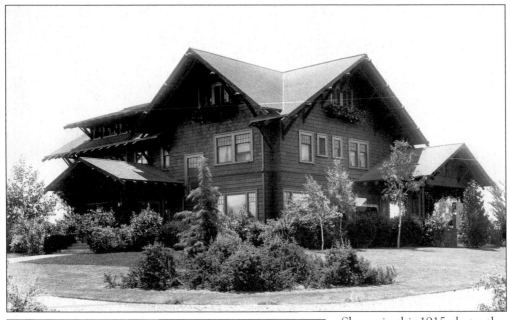

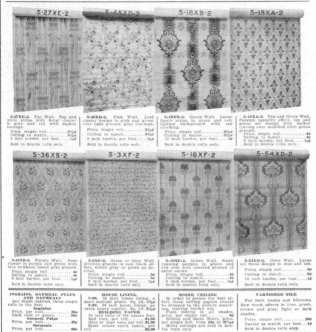

Shown in this 1915 photo, the Breuner family home at Forty-first and Folsom was an exceptional example of the Craftsman style with a low-pitched, gabled roof, wide eave overhang, exposed rafters, and decorative braces under the gables. The house, constructed about 1915, was torn down to make way for a high rise apartment building.

Wallpaper became a popular feature in homes. Wright and Kimbrough offered it for new homes, and Breuner's 1914 catalog offered it for those who wished to update their homes in the latest style.

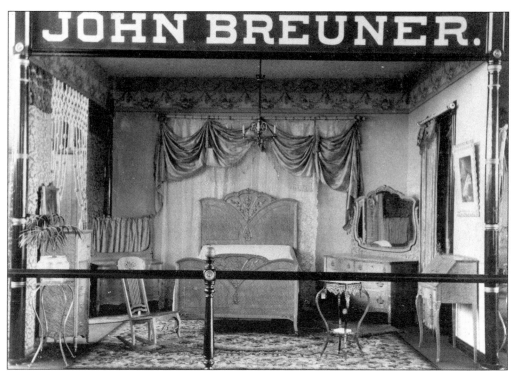

Interior exhibits at the California State Fair in 1895 illustrate the parlor and bedroom furnishings supplied by Breuner Furniture to East Sacramento homes.

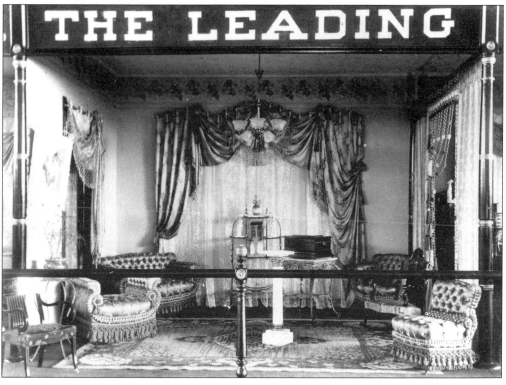

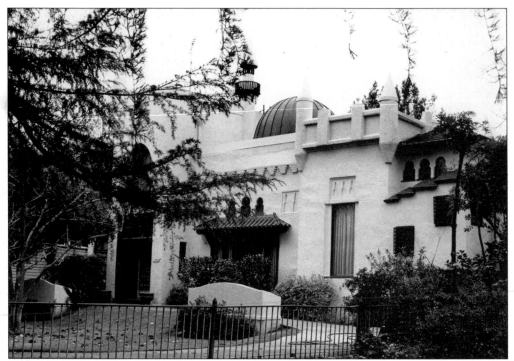

The Lubin house on Thirty-ninth Street was distinctive with its Moorish arches. S.J. Lubin was vice president and secretary of Weinstock & Lubin department store.

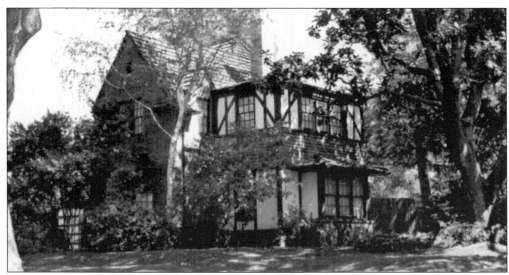

This home has stood on Fortieth Street since 1918, representing Tudor-style construction with steep roof and half-timbering. D.A. and Claire Cannon paid $10,000 for their Dean & Dean home and lived there from 1921 to 1959. (Photo by Barbara Smith Eychaner, 2004.)

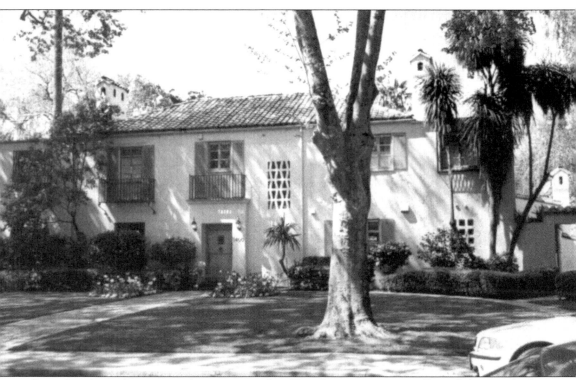

Spanish eclectic homes are also represented in East Sacramento, typically with low-pitched roofs, arched doorways, asymmetrical design, stucco exterior, and red tile roof. This Dean & Dean home on Fortieth Street was purchased for $12,000 in 1925 by William S. Hart. (Photo by Barbara Smith Eychaner, 2004.)

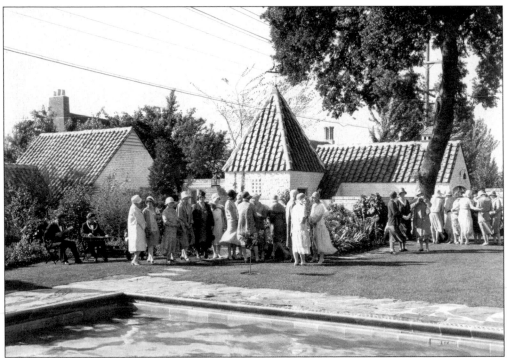

Mrs. Pollock entertained the American Society of Civil Engineers at a garden party in April 1930 at her home on Forty-fifth Street. George Pollock's construction company contributed significantly to local and national projects, including sewer construction for Sacramento; a five-mile stretch of the All-American canal, the 80-mile-long irrigation canal serving the Imperial Valley; and, in 1937, when most of the Navy's fleet had been transferred to the Pacific, a $3.5 million graving dock at Mare Island.

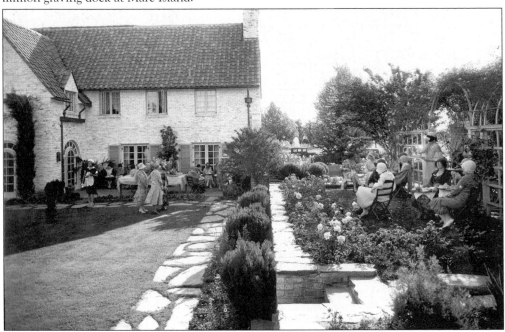

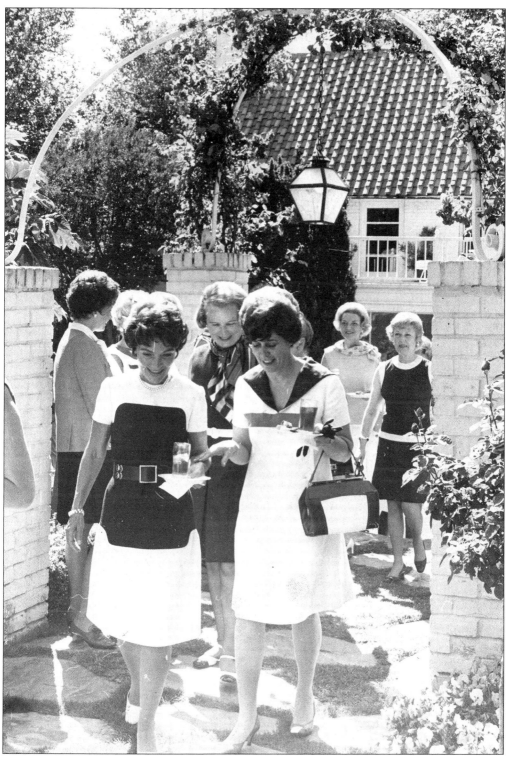

Nancy Reagan also entertained at the Pollock home in May 1970.

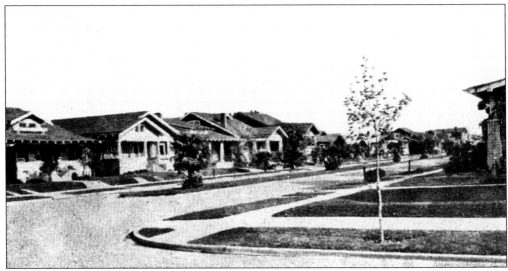

The homes on McCullough Avenue (Dolores Way), Wright and Kimbrough Tract 25, attracted families with their proximity to the streetcar line, only a 15-minute ride from downtown. A down payment of $250 would buy a five-room bungalow that featured a living room fireplace with clinker brick, dining room with built-in bookcases, buffet, elm-paneled walls, and electrical fixtures. Terraced yards added elevation making the second-story flood-house style unnecessary.

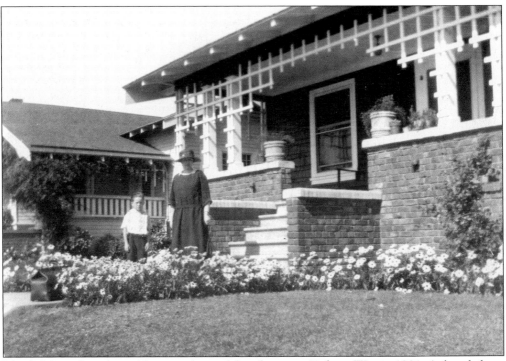

Maude Matteoli and son Al pose in front of their home on Dolores Way in 1921. A decade later Sacramento Circle #150 of the United Ancient Order of Druids chose Maude as its new arch-druidess; she was also a member of the Daughters of Italy.

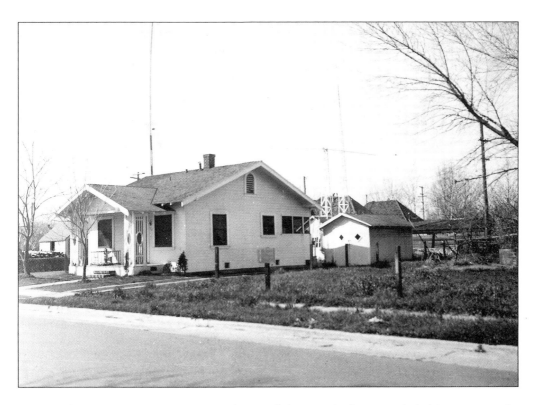

A modest home constructed in 1924 on Thirty-eighth Street for $2,200 included four rooms and a garage. The home saw several occupants in its first few years, including a salesman, a carpenter, and an operator for Pacific Gas & Electric. At times it was vacant. A room was added in 1948, a new detached garage in 1955. By 1959 the Galvins had moved in and stayed for more than 30 years. The house is shown above in 1938 and below in 2004. (Bottom photo by Barbara Smith Eychaner.)

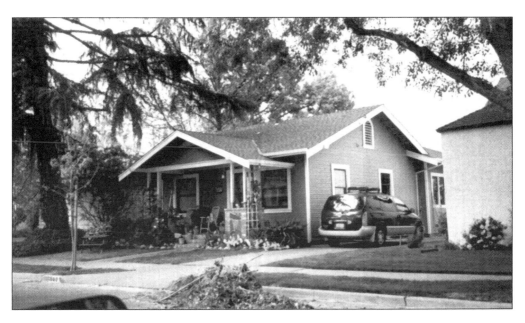

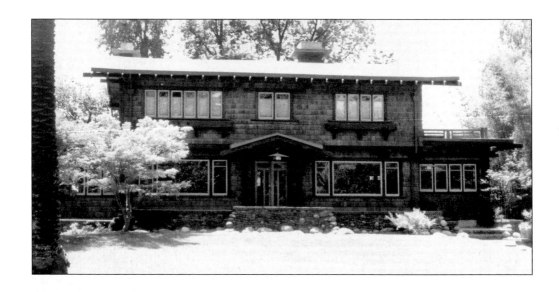

Unlike modest homes, those designed by architects were more detailed. The rounded corners on the beams and braces of this Craftsman-style home on H Street, designed by the noted architects Charles Sumner Greene and Henry Mather Greene, give the illusion of having been assembled with wooden pegs. Developer John T. Greene had the home built as part of an upscale development immediately south of McKinley Park. (Top photo courtesy of Barbara Smith Eychaner, 2004; bottom photo courtesy of Kerry Phillips, 2000.)

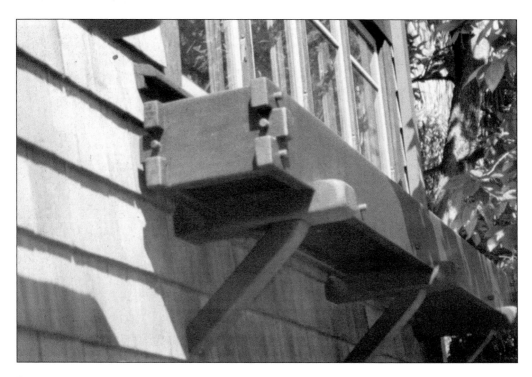

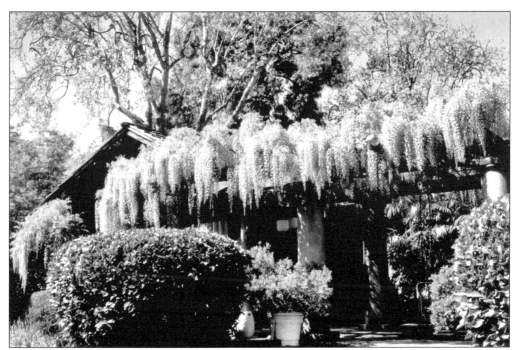

The Haw house on Thirty-ninth Street remains essentially unchanged from the time it was built about 1918. The home boasts redwood siding, treated with palm oil applied at construction, and since then has not been painted or treated in any other way. The architect remains a mystery, but the home possesses elements common to both Greene & Greene and Julia Morgan. (Top photo courtesy of Carson Hendricks, 2004; bottom photo courtesy of Kerry Phillips, 1998.)

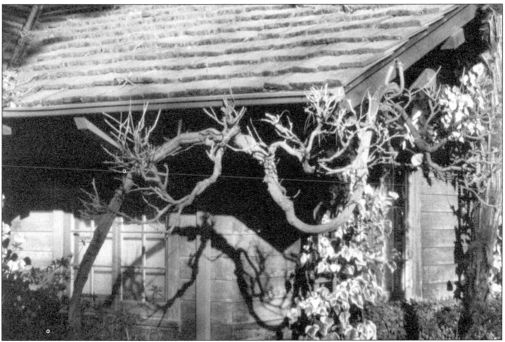

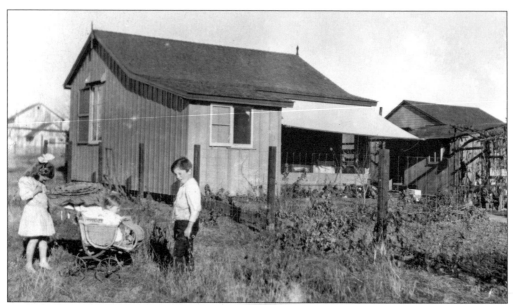

The Mellor family and some of their neighbors on G Street built shacks at the rear of their property for use while their homes were under construction. Pictured here are Hilda, Rose, and Arthur c. 1912. Rose, born in the shack, lived at this property for 91 years, from 1911 to 2002.

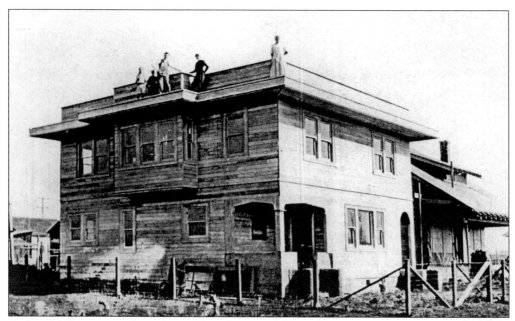

Arthur Mellor, pictured on the roof in this 1914 photo, was a manual training instructor at David Lubin School, perhaps more qualified than most to attempt his own home construction. Completion of the home, however, was delayed after Arthur fell from the second story into the basement.

Mrs. Mellor and her children—Eunice, Ruby, Winnie, Arthur, Hilda, Conrad, and Rose—enjoy dinner in the shack c. 1913.

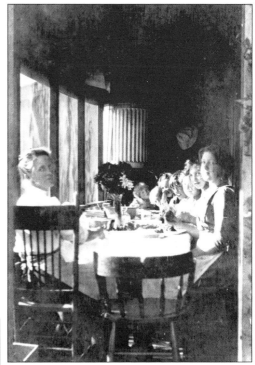

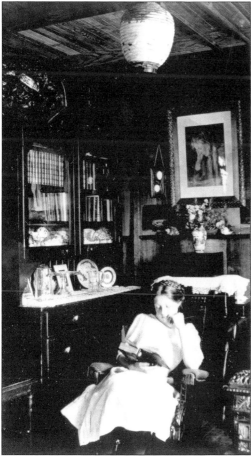

Hilda Mellor enjoys some quiet time inside the shack in this 1914 photo. Notice the Chinese lantern and the well-stocked library.

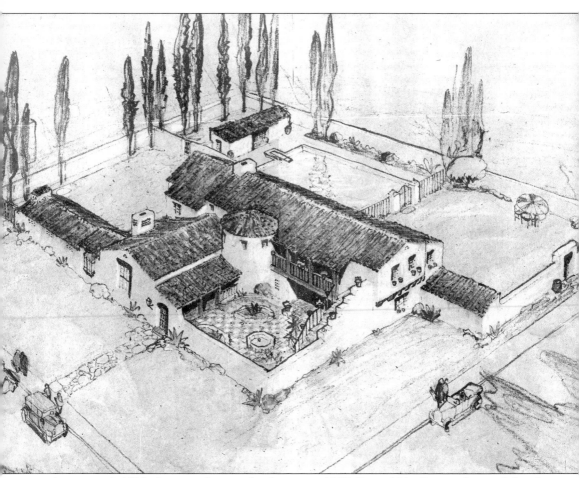

An original 1925 drawing depicts the home at 1225 Forty-fifth Street, designed by the preeminent architectural team of Sacramento in the early 20th century, Charles and James Dean. The home's first owner, J.J. Jacobs, was a successful Buick, Cadillac, and LaSalle representative. The home was constructed in 1926 at a cost of $50,000.

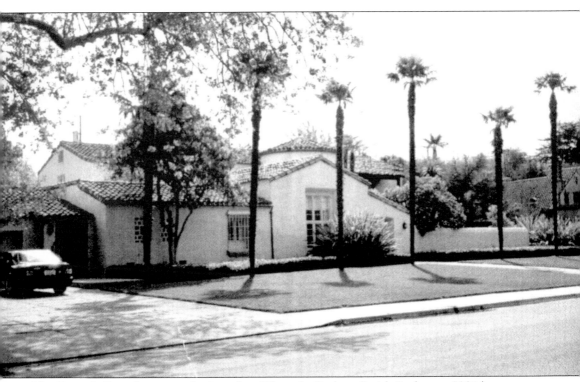

The Dean & Dean home as it looks today. (Photo by Barbara Smith Eychaner, 2004.)

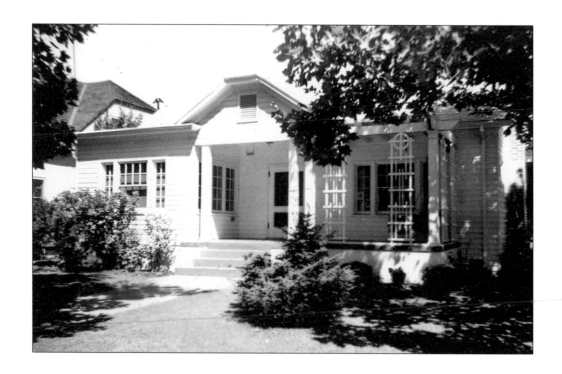

The first home of Edgar and Fern Sayre, shown in 1942 (above) and again in 2004 (below), has undergone a major remodel. Many homes in East Sacramento are considered small by today's standards, and additions and remodels are not unusual. (Bottom photo by Barbara Smith Eychaner.)

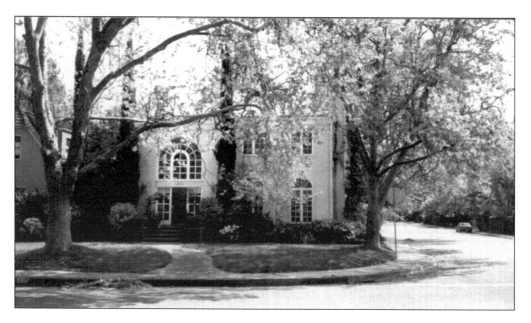

Three

FACES OF
EAST SACRAMENTO
BY DEBBIE POULSEN

The story of East Sacramento is not complete without an exploration of the many families that have either made their lives in the area or merely sojourned there for a time. Far from being a monolithic homogeneous community, East Sacramento families reflect the economic and social diversity of the larger city. From its initial platting in 1908, prominent businessmen, lawyers, doctors, and real estate agents flocked to buy and build homes there. Various immigrant families were also able to find modest housing available in East Sacramento, and most were able to rent or buy homes. These newcomers all enjoyed pleasant neighborhoods, good schools, parks, churches, and all of the new modern inventions such as electric lighting and telephones.

It is through the stories of East Sacramento families that we can come to appreciate the integration of the community into the larger city. East Sacramento families enjoyed their city, as evidenced by the stories of Marilyn Meister Hanson, who grew up in East Sacramento in the 1920s and 1930s. Marilyn's mother had few worries of her children heading downtown to see movies at the theaters on K Street. Movies were always deemed appropriate, and teenagers could ride the J Street trolley to go downtown. Saturday matinees were a popular form of entertainment for the youth, and streetcar fares and admission tickets were inexpensive. In the 1930s, Nancy O'Neil Donahue, raised on Forty-third Street, remembered going downtown and talking to people, as it was still a small town atmosphere where people knew each other. Nancy recalled that her block was filled with 63 children who undoubtedly enjoyed a wonderful and active childhood, playing kick-the-can and other such activities.

Families also helped shape the physical design of East Sacramento. In addition to building their own homes, they planted the many distinguished and beautiful trees that currently line the streets, many now over 80 feet tall. Rose (Mellor) Millward once related an interesting story about a young couple, John and Ida Jennings, who lived at 4465 G Street. Rose's family, as well as the Jennings, had emigrated from Ambleside, England. About 1910, when John sent for Ida to come to East Sacramento to live, she found that she missed the trees and birds she had been so fond of back home. One day while walking to catch the streetcar on J Street, she found an English Oak acorn. Ida carried it around in her pocket for a time as a reminder of her homeland. When pregnant with her first child, she planted the acorn in their backyard. It grew for many years and still stands today.

There are stories for each family of East Sacramento. Every family and individual has played an important role in developing the community into a great place to live and raise children. In no way are the photographs that follow a portrayal of all families that have made East Sacramento their home. Indeed, they capture only a glimpse into family life. We have tried to provide a cross-section of the many families that have lived here and to capture the true character of the community.

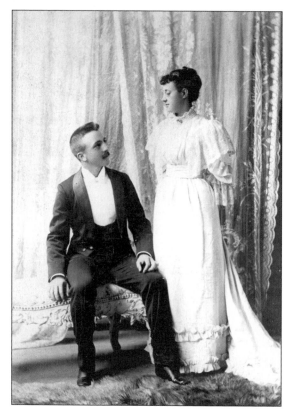

Louis Frederick and Clara (Schmidt) Breuner were married on June 14, 1893. They later made their home at 1128 Forty-fifth Street. Louis, prominent in the furniture business and as a civic leader, was a widower when he died in 1947, at the age of 78 years.

John and Ida Elizabeth Jennings emigrated to Sacramento from England. In 1910, upon finding an English oak-tree acorn on the way to catch the streetcar on J Street, Mrs. Jennings planted it in their backyard at Forty-fourth and G Street. The tree still stands. They are pictured here in their shack.

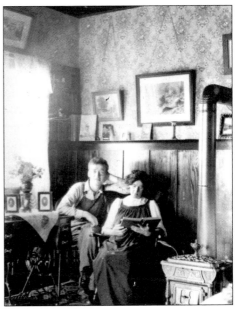

In the early 1910s at McKinley Park, Margaret Buell and her friend Vernal Rodda rode the swing. Vernal was born in 1890 and lived on Forty-fourth Street with his wife, Olive, and family for most of his life. He was one of several brothers who operated three pharmacies under the name of Rodda Brothers.

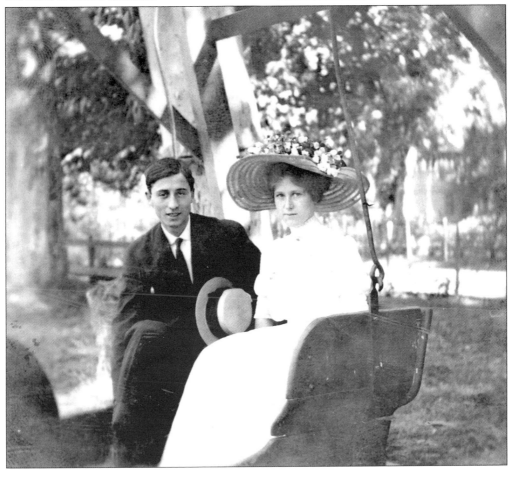

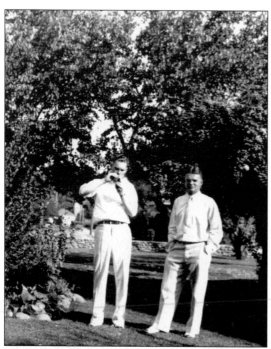

Dwight Miller and an unidentified friend courted Margaret and Dorothy Meister in the early 1920s. Dwight eventually married Dorothy. (Photo courtesy of Marilyn Meister Hanson.)

Playing on the lodge pole swing in McKinley Park c. 1915 are Tom Richards, Wesley Thomas, George Bovey, Elsie Elizabeth (Rule) Bovey, and Myrtle Hausman. George was a butcher and had just married Elsie. They lived at 3430 L Street for many years.

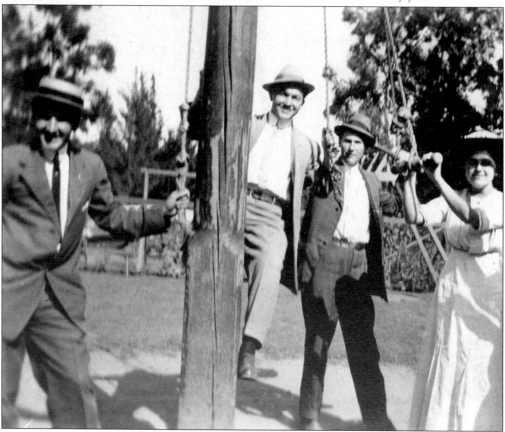

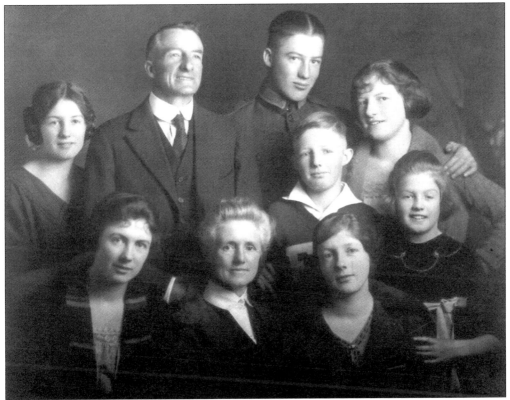

The Mellor family pose in 1920. Seated, from left to right, are Ruby, Bernice, Eunice, and Rose. Standing, from left to right, are Hilda, Arthur, Art, Conrad, and Winifred. Rose Mellor (Millward) qualified third in the nation in the high jump for the 1932 Olympics. The Breuners offered to sponsor her, but she declined, as Babe Didrikson (Zaharias), who set the world record, was also competing.

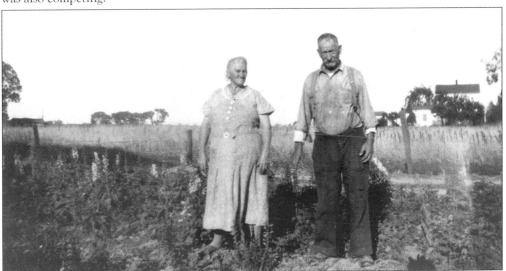

Mr. and Mrs. Cecchettini are pictured at the ranch by Forty-fifth and B Street in the 1930s. This is now Bertha Henshell Park. The Miliken home can be seen in the background.

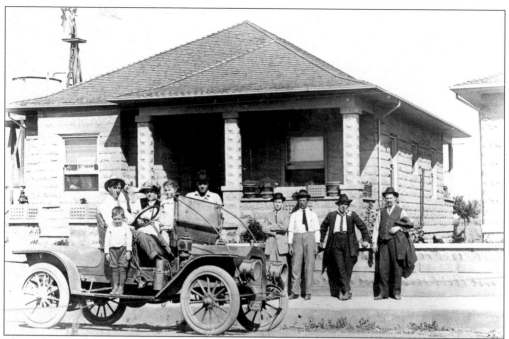

The Fifty-second and M Street home of Fred and his brother Primo Belluomini was made of stones quarried from East Portal Park, c. 1915. Fred married Iva M. Gerken in June 1923 after meeting at the Capitol National Bank where they both worked.

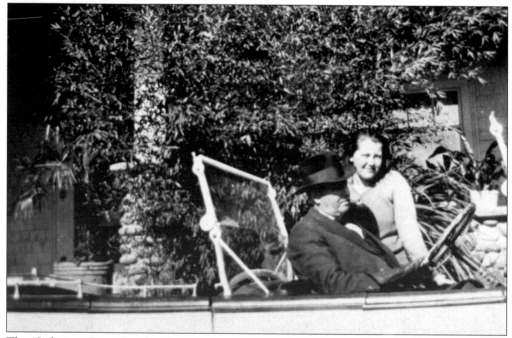

The "Infamous Boat Car," made by Albert R. Meister, had brass rails and a boat tail rear end. Albert's wife Ethel thought the car was "too fancy" and did not like to ride in it. Daughter Margaret, who later became a local schoolteacher, is shown as a teenager with her father, Albert, at the helm. (Photo courtesy of Marilyn Meister Hanson.)

Ethel Flaherty Meister enjoys a quiet afternoon in her garden with the family's "police" dog, Hundun, in this *c.* 1930 photo. (Photo courtesy of Marilyn Meister Hanson.)

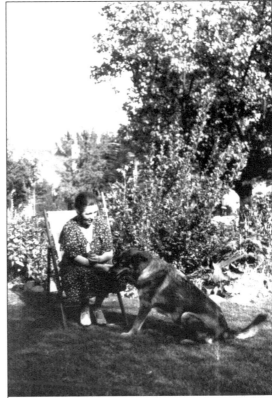

Pictured here, from left to right, is the Giuseppe Pane family: Giuseppe, Joe, Julio, and Rosina; (back row) Larry, Orlie, Theresa, John, and Pat. Giuseppe worked for the railroad as a machinist and tinsmith at this time, *c.* 1925. The family home was on Fifty-fifth Street.

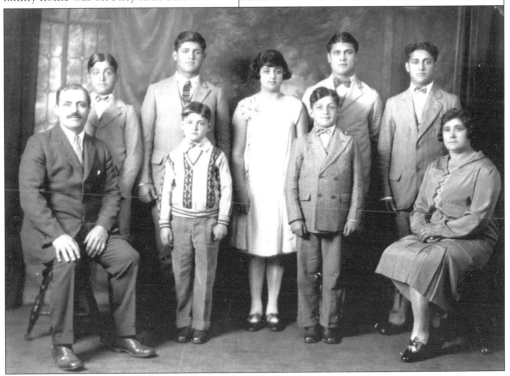

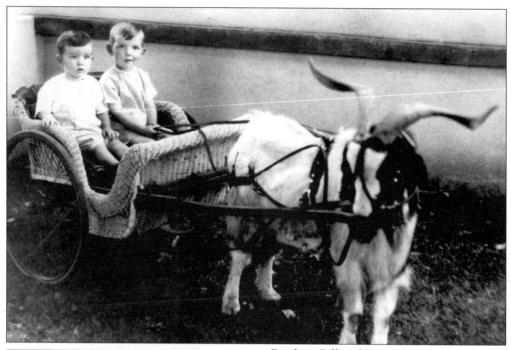

Brothers Bill and Tim Kennedy played in a wicker cart pulled by a black and white goat with long horns. This was taken at 3010 H Street, *c.* 1927.

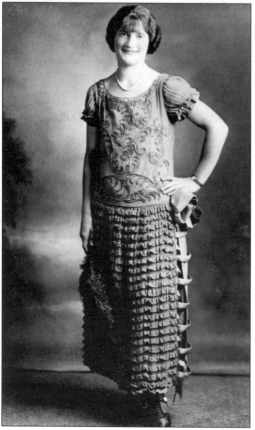

Shown in this *c.* 1924 photo, stylish Henrietta Inderkum (Jansen) was the daughter of Joseph Inderkum, a local Swiss German dairyman. The family lived at Fortieth and J Streets. She later worked as a nurse at Mercy General Hospital and lived on T Street.

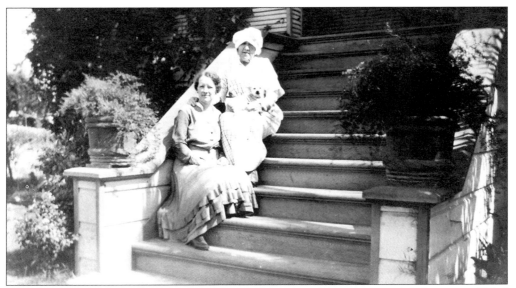

Relaxed on the steps of the Simpson home between Thirty-ninth and I Street are Ethel Simpson Beach and Annie Rogers Simpson, c. 1917.

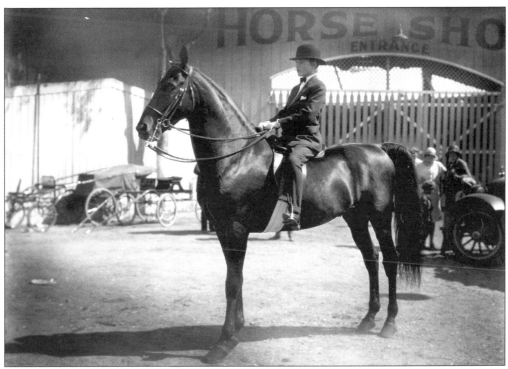

Barbara Worth rode Waveland's Choice at the age of 14 at the California State Fair, c. 1926. This was the first time Barbara wore her new riding habit. It was the beginning of an incredible career of hunter-jumping horse training. Her mother and stepfather Bert Brown, a horse shoer and trainer, lived and owned stables at 4615 B Street.

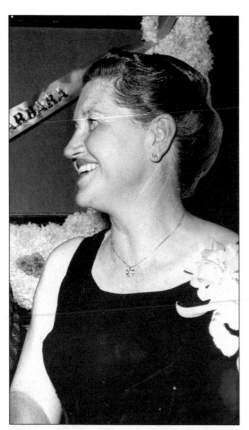

A farewell party was held at the Governor's Hall on the State Fair Grounds in 1963 for well-known Sacramento horsewoman and riding-school operator Barbara Worth. She was voted the AHSA Horsewoman of the Year in 1962, which she considered a milestone in her career. In 1994 she was inducted into the Show Jumping Hall of Fame.

Mabel and John Bone gave out free milkshakes at People's Drugstore when the local team won football games. The Bones were well known for their caring service at the popular hangout. Shown in the 1930s are John, Mabel, and Mrs. Parsons, who was the first teacher at Theodore Judah School.

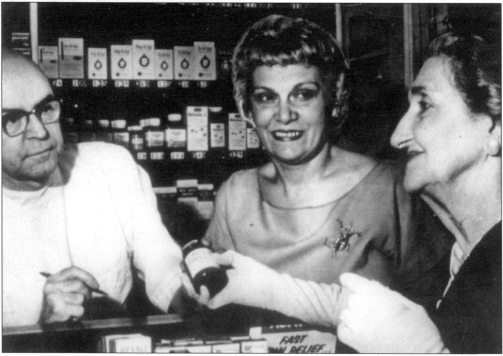

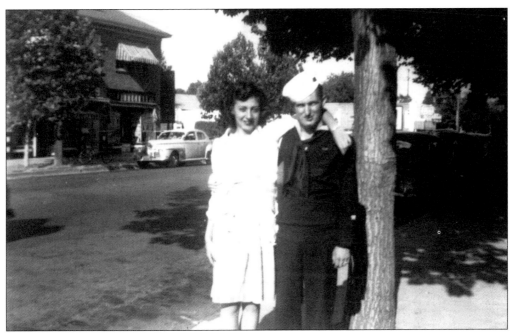

Delina Da Prato Skarles and Carlo Morey pose on July 2, 1943. The picture was taken at Forty-seventh and Forty-eight on J Street.

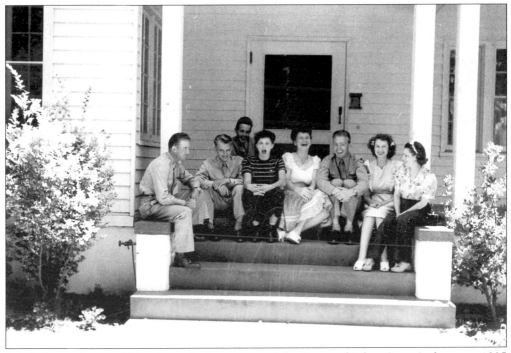

Labeled as a picture of friends on the front steps of the Fern and Edgar Sayre Jr. home at 1235 Forty-second Street, this photo was probably sent to Ed during World War II. From left to right are Lieutenant Norris, Sid, Chester, Sissy, Shirley, Lieutenant Dickerson, Maxine, and Fern Sayre. Chester was on furlough, soon to be married.

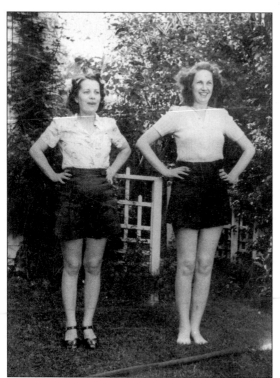

Fern R. (Sammis) Sayre, wife of Edgar Sayre Jr., and friend Maxine do their exercises in Fern's backyard on Forty-second Street. Ed served as a private in the Army 159th Infantry, stationed on the Aleutian Islands, *c.* 1943.

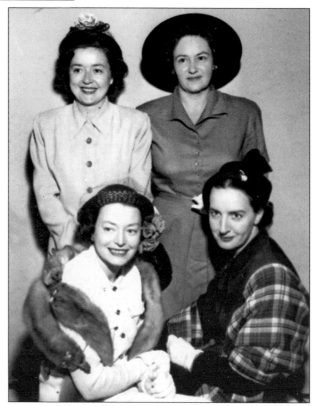

Shown are members of the Sacred Heart Mother's Club, taken April 4, 1951. Seated, from left to right, are Mrs. Jack (Dorothy) Steiner and Mrs. James Gerry; standing are Mrs. Lou Warren and Mrs. Walter (Dorothy) Chester.

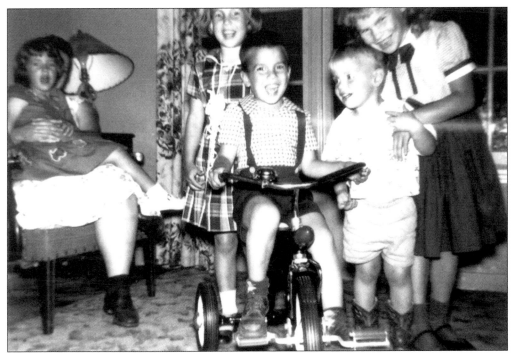

In the Elvas District, Stephen Shaltes loved his third birthday when he received a new tricycle on May 9, 1957! Seated are his mother, Carol, and cousin Pamela Oldham. The Shaltes children, Susan, Stephen, Craig (note the cowboy boots), and Kathleen, enjoy this day with their brother. (Photo courtesy Erwin and Carol Shaltes.)

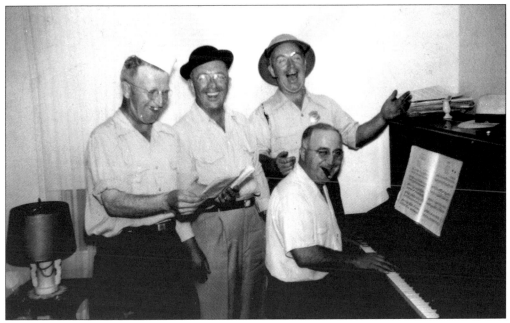

Four Irish O'Hare brothers sing together in 1960. From left to right are John, James, Pat, and Michael (seated at the piano). Michael worked for the railroad and lived on Dolores Street.

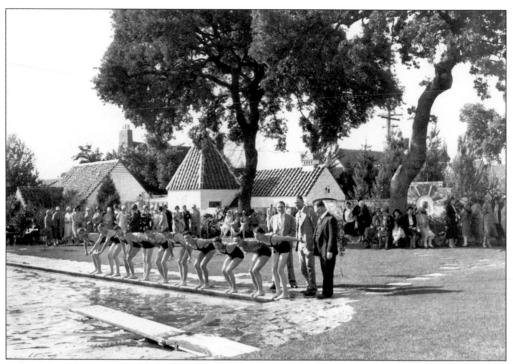

Swimmers prepare to enter the pool at a Pollock garden party *c*. 1930.

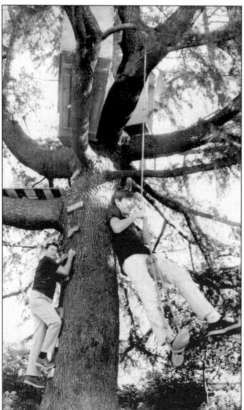

In this photo taken on November 15, 1971, Gov. Ronald Reagan and son Ronald Jr. ("Skip") play in the treehouse at the yard on 1341 Forty-fifth Street. The family rented the former residence of George Pollock while Reagan served as governor.

Four

GOOD OLD GOLDEN RULE DAYS

By Candis R. Sieg

The sounds of high-buttoned shoes clattering across the fences and fields of East Sacramento could be heard every morning as children ran from their homes to the one-room schoolhouse on J Street in the 1890s. As Sacramento began to expand into the hinterland, many businessmen chose to move their families out of the bustling center of Sacramento and into large farmhouses in East Sacramento. The first school in the area was simply named East Sacramento School after the area it served. Eventually, the one-room schoolhouse developed into a two-story, two-room schoolhouse, making it easier for the teacher to ring the school bell in the morning.

As more families moved into the area, the demand for qualified teachers increased, and many local young women began to pursue careers in education. In some cases, lack of qualified teachers was not a problem, but finding a suitable school building was. This was the case at the Theodore Judah School that opened in 1927. It was opened as a temporary two-room bungalow and was not funded to become a public school until ten years later. Today, it is listed on the National Register of Historic Places. Other schools such as the Elmhurst Elementary School were packed beyond capacity in the 1920s, and students used recycled crates as desks and folding auditorium chairs for the kindergarten class. Jobs in education became scarce during the depression of the 1930s. Even though the average annual salary for an elementary school teacher was only $1,500, there was an abundance of qualified teachers, and any who held a position as a teacher savored it.

As children in the area approached high school age, they were sent to Oak Park to Sacramento High School. Those who went on to higher education stayed in the Oak Park area attending Sacramento City College. That changed in 1953 with the opening of California State University, Sacramento. At the time, Sacramento State College, as it was called, was geared to attract lower-income families. In fact, many of the enrolling students were single mothers and those from rural backgrounds.

The college construction was finished behind schedule, and the new university president Dr. West, vice president Dr. Walker, and their wives realized two nights before the school opening that the room numbers had not yet been painted on the doors. The foursome spent December 31 making impromptu room numbers out of cardboard and felt tip pens. Working into the next day, the couples taped the numbers to each door on the campus.

At the opening ceremony, 150 automobiles drove west from the old City College in Oak Park to the new Sacramento State College campus at 6000 J Street. The campus was described as a dustbowl, although the first few years it became a boggy marsh in the rain. Later, nothing was worse then the abundance of jackrabbits that devoured any vegetation the groundskeepers had put in. After the second set of infant greenery was destroyed, the groundskeepers called upon the community to take up arms, leading to the Great Jack Rabbit Massacre of 1953. The campus today is alive with students and is described as a destination campus in California. Chickens still roam the campus freely.

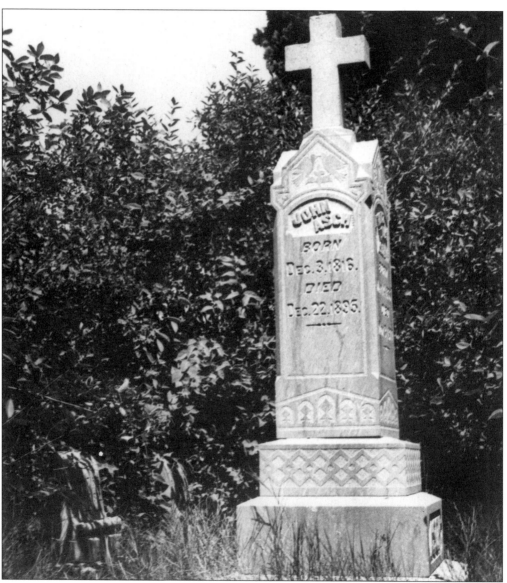

This grave marker, formerly located in the New Helvetia Cemetery at the corner of Thirty-first and J Street, has been removed to make way for Sutter Middle School. All markers were removed to either the city cemetery or East Lawn Cemetery.

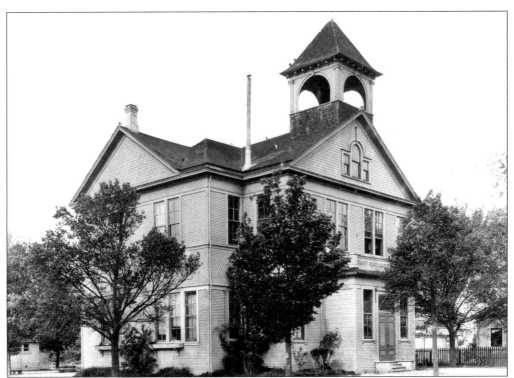

The East Sacramento School was located on the southwest corner of Thirty-ninth and J Streets. Taken in 1923, this picture shows the second-story addition. The school later became the Sacred Heart of Jesus Church. In recent years the school has been made into a private Christian school; the original schoolhouse became a gym.

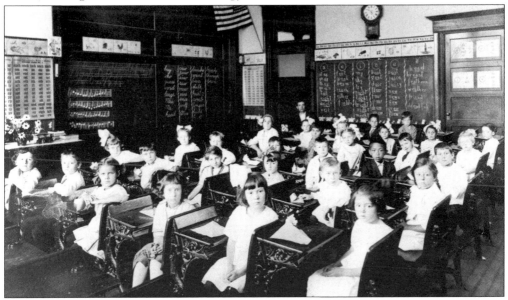

Third graders at McKinley Elementary School in 1914 practiced cursive writing, spelling, and music on the blackboards. Among the class, composed of East Sacramento residents, there was only one Asian student, pictured here in the third row.

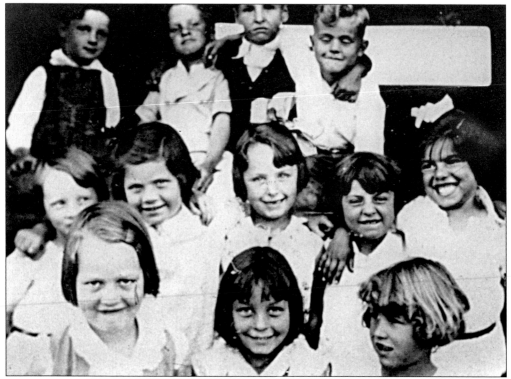

In this 1927 photo, not everyone smiled in the first class at Theodore Judah Elementary School. One student commented that the children in Theodore Judah were teased by those from David Lubin because the school was composed of temporary shacks.

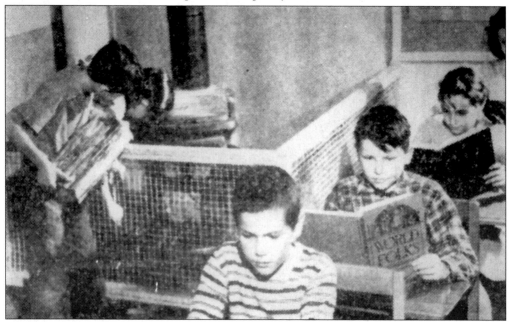

Starting as small two-room bungalows, or shacks as many of the students called them, the Theodore Judah classrooms used woodburning stoves to provide heat in the early 1950s.

The principal of Theodore Judah School planted a redwood tree in the late 1920s. The redwood towers over the school today with a diameter of over three feet at the base.

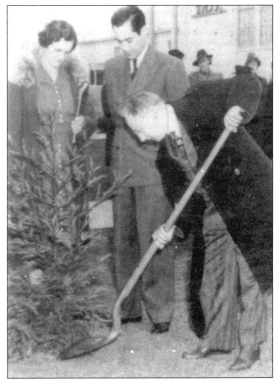

The sixth grade class at Theodore Judah School sat for their picture in 1958.

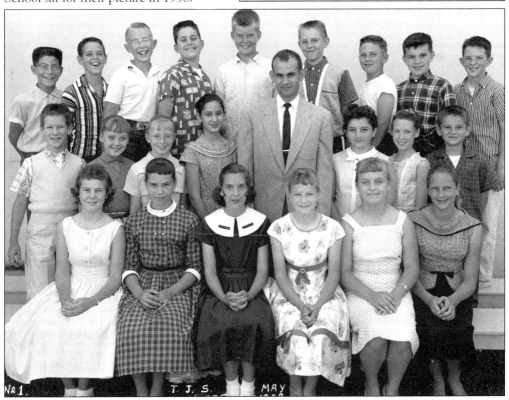

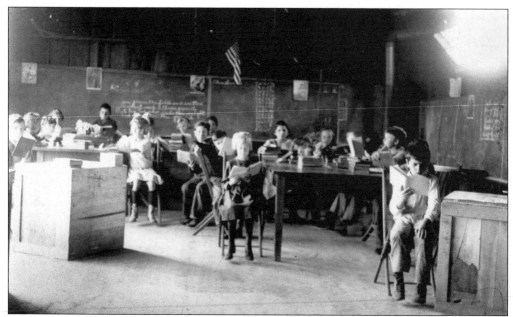

The Elmhurst Kindergarten Class in 1921 used recycled shipping crates as desks. The school later changed its name to Coloma School.

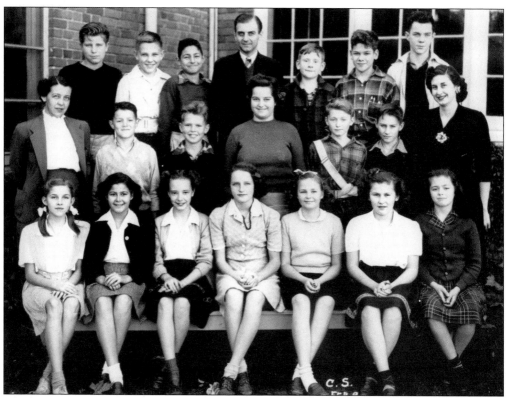

Teacher Margaret Meister and her class pose for the annual school picture at Coloma School in February 1948.

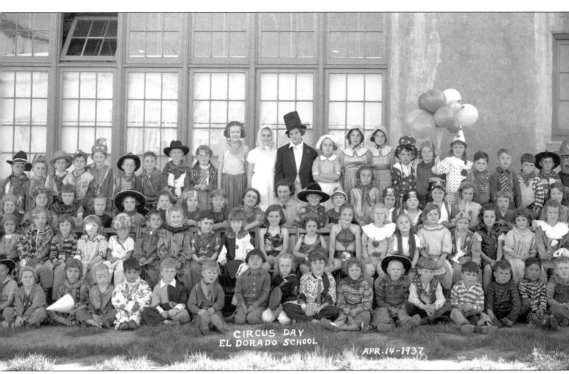

Cowboys, clowns, and ringmasters walked the halls of the El Dorado School on Circus Day. This photo, taken April 14, 1937, is of the entire student body. Those who could come to school in costume did; those who could not still shared in the fun of seeing their classmates dressed up.

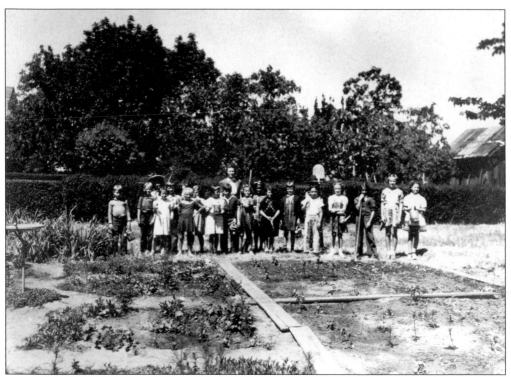

Students of El Dorado School pose proudly with tools they used to work in their garden in 1937. Boards were put in as walkways throughout the garden to prevent damaging the plants. The garden project continues today at the David Lubin School.

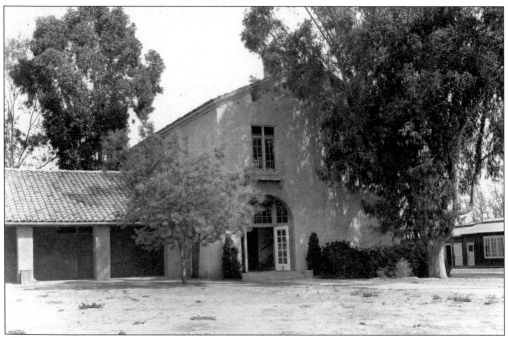

This photo shows the entrance to El Dorado School in 1930.

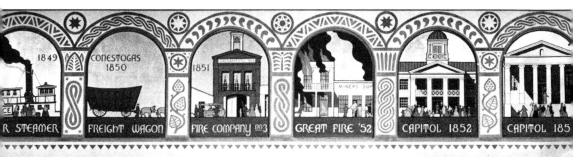

The Kit Carson School decorated their walls in celebration of history in the area. In the auditorium, 15 murals representing significant historical events of early Sacramento were painted by artist Earl Barnett in 1974.

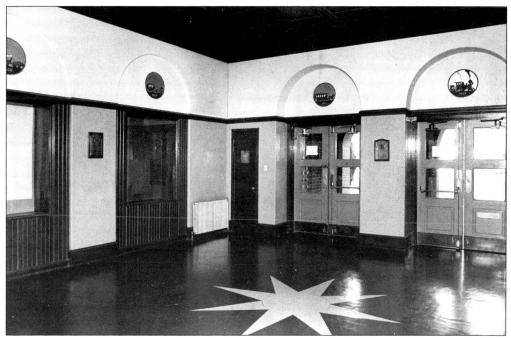

The hallway in Kit Carson School housed four of the six plaques also painted by Earl Barnet. All plaques represented a mode of early transportation. The new school cost $300,000 to build in 1933.

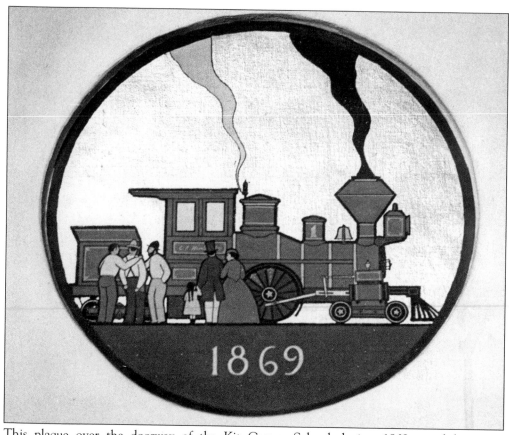

This plaque over the doorway of the Kit Carson School depicts 1869 travel by steam locomotive. The picture is one of six in the entryway. Other plaques include an ox cart representing travel in 1830, a stage coach for 1850, a horse-drawn streetcar in 1861, the locomotive in 1869, the luxury carriage in 1875, and finally the electric streetcar in 1888.

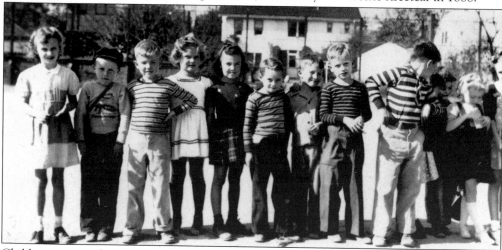

Children pose on the playground at the David Lubin School in 1942. The David Lubin School was built to accommodate the students transferred from the old East Sacramento School. The school is located near Thirty-sixth and M Streets.

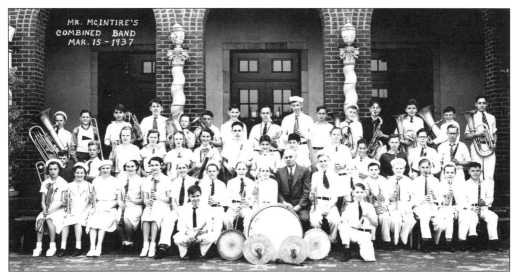

Children could toot their own horns or march to the beat of their own drummers in Mr. McIntire's combined band from Kit Carson Junior High School. The students pose in March 1937 with instruments in hand.

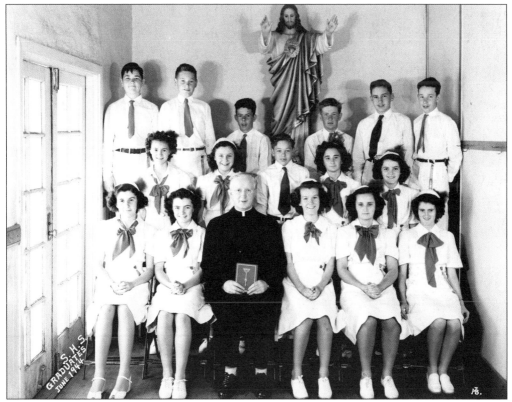

The Sacred Heart School was once the East Sacramento School in the early 1900s. The class picture, taken in 1944 in front of an image of Jesus, shows the importance of religion at the school. Classes were taught by priests or nuns, and included confirmation preparation in their eighth-grade classes.

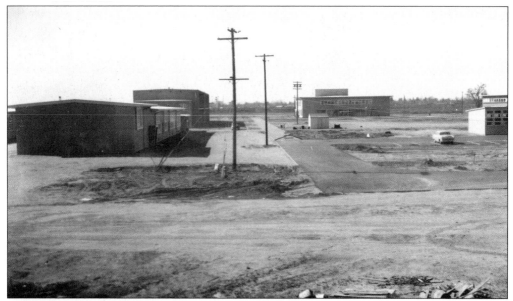

Taken at the J Street entrance of the new Sacramento State College in February 1953, this picture shows how barren the campus was before the "Great Jack Rabbit Massacre." When the school opened, a parade of 150 automobiles drove from the old city college to the new Sacramento State College.

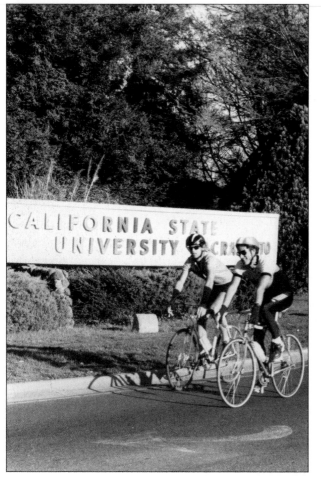

What a change! Two students ride bicycles in front of the entrance sign to Sacramento State in 1995. This similar angle to the 1953 picture shows the campus is no longer barren. Large trees, shrubs, and lush green grass now thrive.

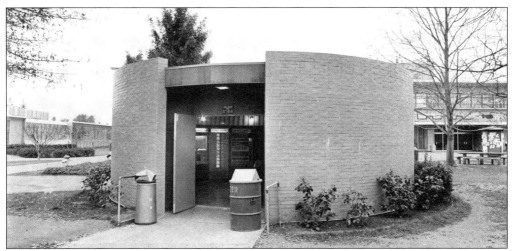

The Round House at Sacramento State was the center of controversy while under construction in 1969. The president at the time allegedly listed curtains in the budget; unfortunately, the Round House has no windows. The curtains purchased somehow found their way into the president's home.

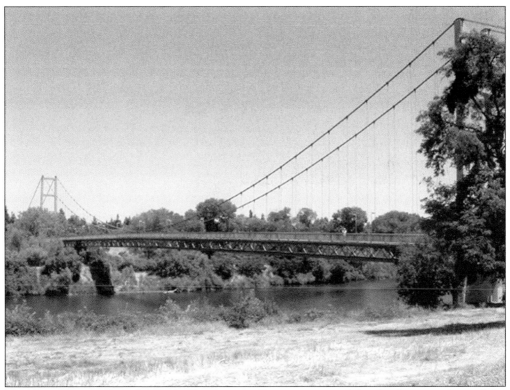

The Guy West walking bridge at Sacramento State was named for the first president of the college. The bridge, shown in 1992, was designed by a physics class at Sacramento State and connects the college to a popular housing section across the American River called Campus Commons.

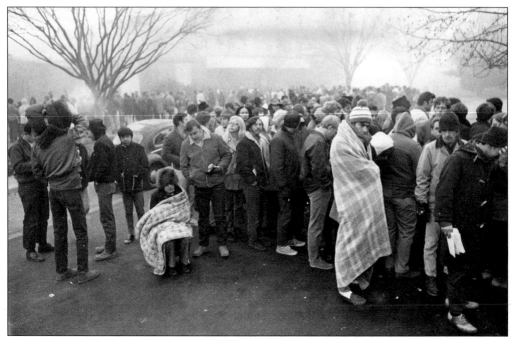

Camping overnight at school was an event every semester. Students waited in line to register at California State College in October 1969. The campus originally registered on a first-come, first-serve basis. Students camped out to rush into the gym the next morning to get the classes they wanted for the next semester.

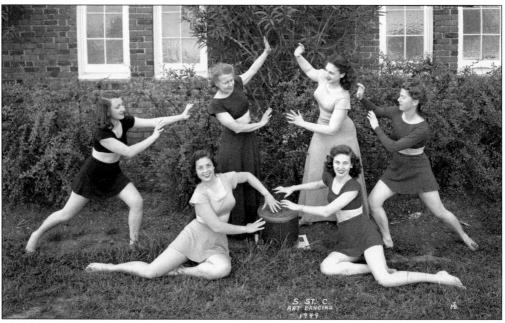

The beat of the drum kept time for the dancers of the art dance class at California State University, Sacramento, in the early 1960s. Students were allowed to show their mid-section, but were forbidden to expose their belly buttons in their costumes.

Five

BUSINESS IS BOOMING
By Lindsay Tateishi

East Sacramento went through many changes throughout the early 20th century as it slowly moved away from a farming community toward a more residential suburb. As the suburb grew, so did its modest commercial area. Businesses began to sprout up along the busy roads of J Street and Folsom Boulevard. Grocery stores, gas stations, and family-run businesses paved the way for a more commercial East Sacramento. Since most businesses were located within walking distance of the residential neighborhoods, many prospered quickly. Two such businesses included Knott's Pharmacy and Crown Cleaners.

Knott's Pharmacy opened in 1938 under the direction of entrepreneur Howard Kessler. Through much hard work, Kessler managed to maintain a pleasant environment for both his staff and his clients. Phyllis Smith, an employee, enjoyed her job so much that she worked there for more than 43 years. Crown Cleaners followed a similar success story. Opened in the late 1890s, Crown Cleaners provided excellent service to its customers for five generations until its demise in the early 21st century.

East Sacramento businesses continue to grow and change. New businesses continue to enter the area with the hopes that their store, too, will prosper as many of the older stores have. Several of the busy streets are now lined with businesses old and new. Although only time will tell which stores will be successful and which will not, one thing remains certain. In East Sacramento, business is booming.

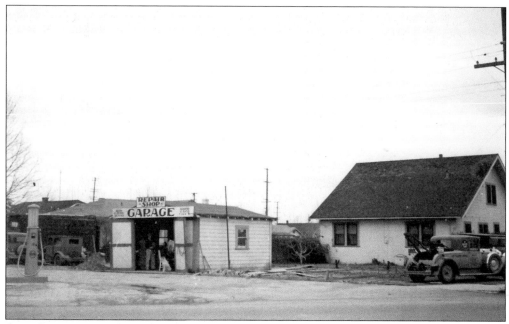

Some businesses, such as this local gas station and repair shop, could be found behind the entrepreneur's home.

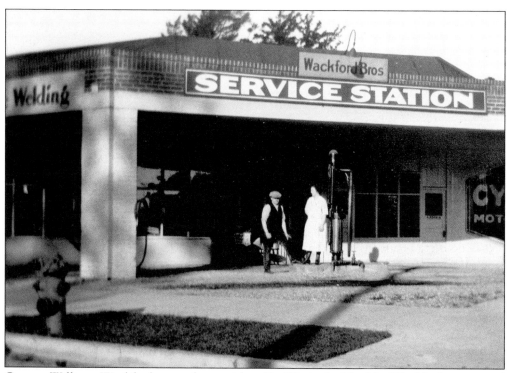

George William Wackford, seen here with wife Elizabeth Matilda Wackford, co-owned the Wackford Brothers Service Station during the 1920s with his brothers Fredrick and William Wackford.

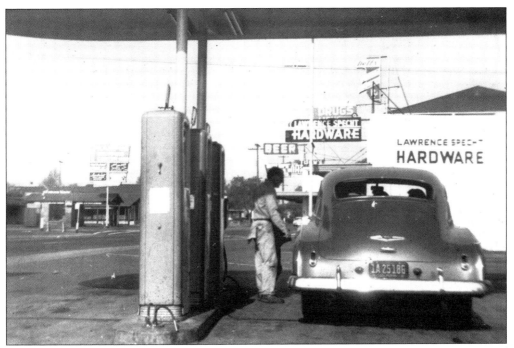

Gas stations such as Duchini's were one form of business that lined the ever-growing streets of East Sacramento.

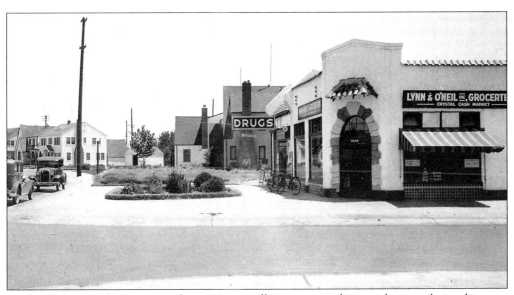

During the early 1930s, businesses still maintained a close relationship to residential neighborhoods as seen in this picture of the corner of McKinley Boulevard and Thirty-sixth Street.

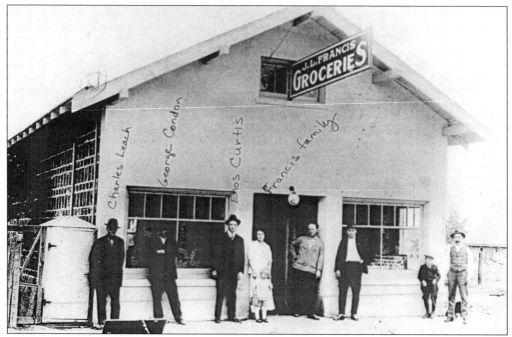

The J.L. Francis grocery store was a family-run business that became a staple of its surrounding community during the early 1920s.

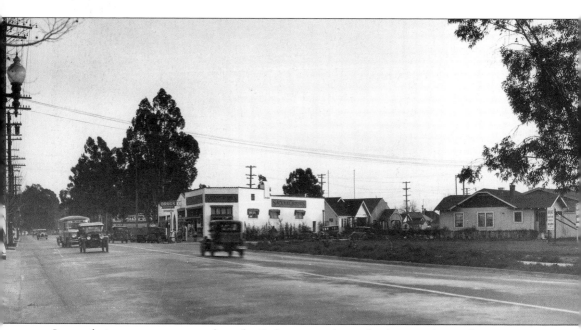

Large chain grocery stores, such as the Safeway seen here, slowly moved into the growing area during the 1940s.

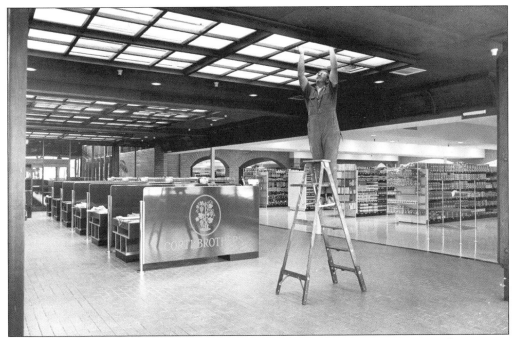

In 1981, Corti Brothers underwent a slight makeover after numerous years of service to help prepare for its grand reopening. This market served the predominately Italian section of East Sacramento.

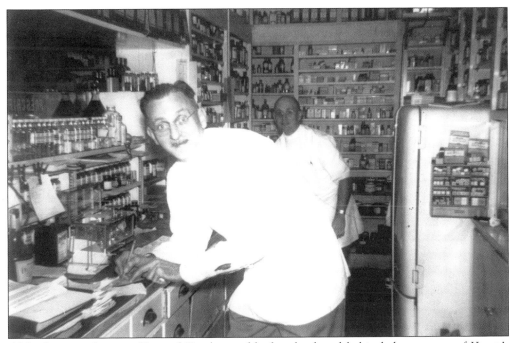

Al Luthring and owner Howard Kessler could often be found behind the counter of Knott's Pharmacy as seen in this photograph from the late 1940s.

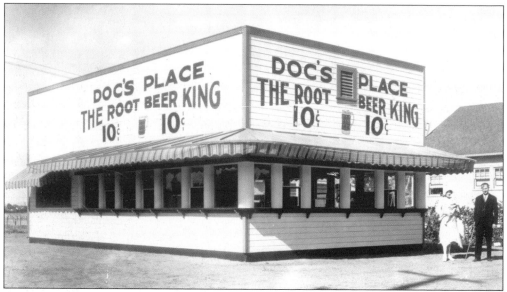

Local businessman Doc Campbell posed with wife Paulette and son Jim in front of his business, Doc's Place.

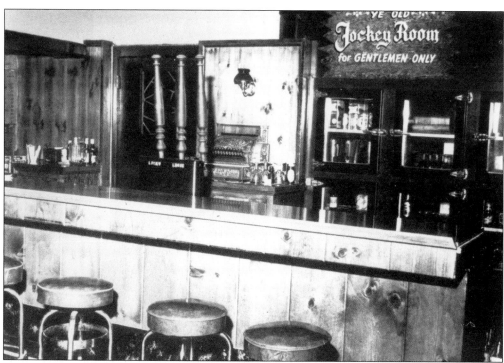

In May 1954, Shakey Johnson founded the original Shakey's pizza parlor at Fifty-seventh and J Streets. Today the building houses the East End Bar and Grill.

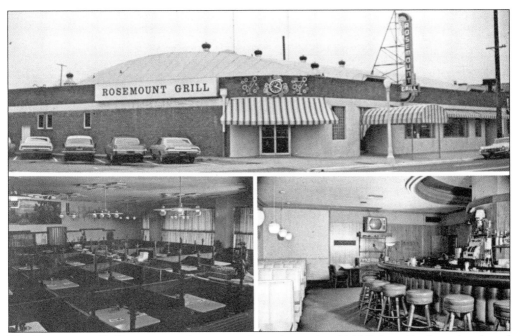

The Rosemount Grill, as seen in this postcard, was located at 3145 Folsom Boulevard and used the slogan "Serving Fine Food to Fine People Since 1914" to help attract new business.

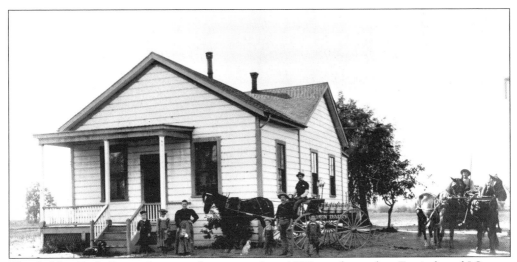

The Golden Eagle Dairy, shown in this picture from 1895, was located on Fortieth and J Streets and served the needs of the growing community.

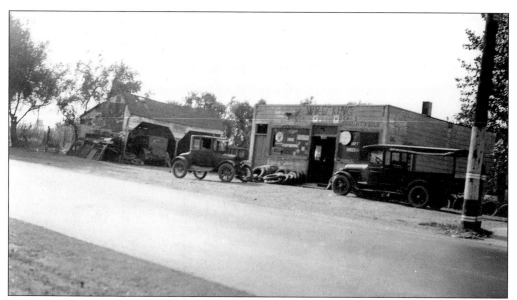

A wide variety of businesses, including this auto-wrecking business located at 5316 Folsom Boulevard, lined the ever-changing streets of East Sacramento, shown in this 1934 photo.

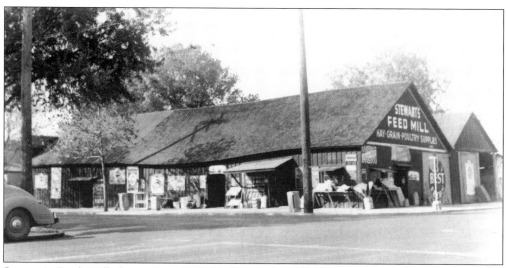

Stewart's Feed Mill, located at 3030 N Street, provided supplies to farmers even as East Sacramento became increasingly residential.

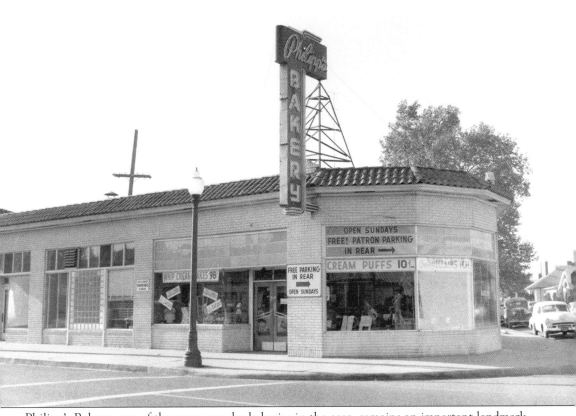

Philipp's Bakery, one of the more popular bakeries in the area, remains an important landmark in the East Sacramento community.

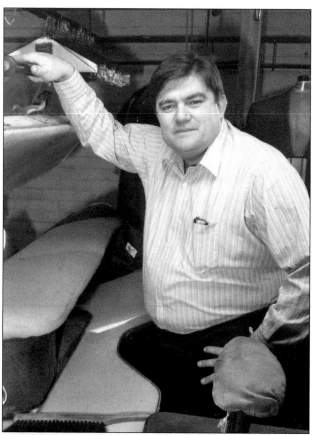

In this 1985 photograph of Crown Cleaners, Don demonstrates the use of a pressing machine.

Owners Larry Robinson and Yvonne Romero pose in 1982 in front of their bicycle accessories store, The Rest Stop.

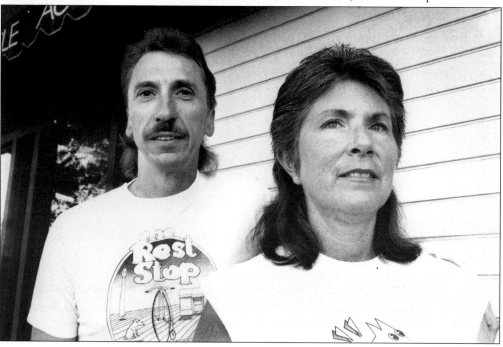

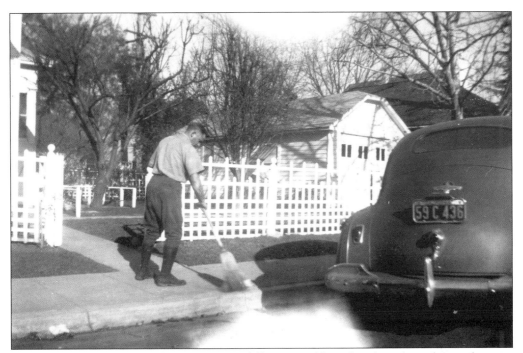

Not everyone worked for a business. Some folks were self-employed, such as this gardener in front of a home on Forty-second Street.

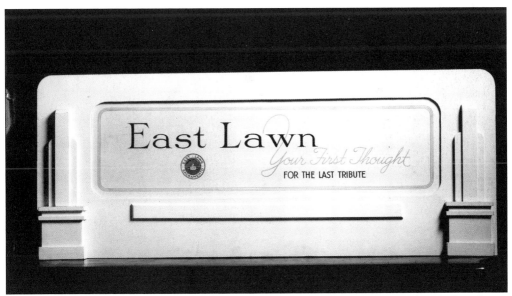

Advertising invaded East Sacramento in the mid-1930s. In this 1937 photo, East Lawn Cemetery advertises its services.

Unlike the cemetery, many businesses, such as the Ing and Allee Company and W.L. Triplett Paper Hanging, chose to advertise their businesses through local annuals.

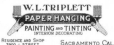

Six

HOW THEY PLAYED

BY AUDRA HAYES

Beginning in the 1860s, the average American work week slowly declined by 20 percent through 1910. With the change in working hours, Americans gained time to play. Like all Americans, East Sacramentans enjoyed recreation. Leisure in this neighborhood demonstrates both a fondness for relaxation and also a sense of pride in the community.

As Sacramento evolved from farmland to concrete and stone, citizens began requesting an area where they could escape from the bustling city. Established in 1871, East Sacramento's East Park filled the bill. One of the first parks in Sacramento, East Park was the creation of the Sacramento Street Railway Company, designed to lure passengers onto the company's trolley, particularly on weekends. As the city's population grew, so did the popularity of the park. In 1902, East Park was renamed McKinley Park and put under the jurisdiction of the city. Due to its importance in the community, many residents helped maintain and upgrade the park. In 1994, citizens helped rejuvenate the park playground. Monetary contributions from the city and private parties, along with labor from more than 2,500 volunteers, built the current McKinley Park Village playground.

As in most American communities, sports have played an important role in connecting the neighborhood. One landmark in the Fabulous Forties is the Sutter Lawn Tennis Club. Established in 1919, the private club drew an enthusiastic response upon its opening. Membership to Sutter Lawn is exclusive. Ronald Regan, who was a member when he lived in the neighborhood, tried to sponsor a friend for a three-month membership but was rejected by the club's board. Not all East Sacramentans could afford to join Sutter Lawn, but residents could find other places to participate in community sports, such as East Portal Park and McKinley Park.

Recreation in East Sacramento has reflected American trends. In the late 1920s, motion pictures became a popular form of entertainment. Across the country, cities built grand movie palaces to showcase the new phenomenon. East Sacramento's opulent movie palace was the Alhambra Theater. Built in 1927, it was considered an architectural and entertainment jewel. Its loss in 1973 continues to be mourned by the community. The pictures in this chapter will show the variety of places and activities where residents have spent their leisure hours.

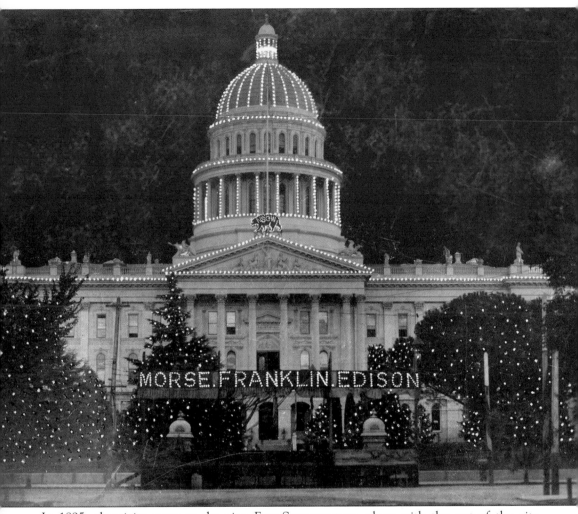

In 1895, electricity came to the city. East Sacramentans, along with the rest of the city, celebrated this technological advancement by decorating street poles and the capital building with strings of lights.

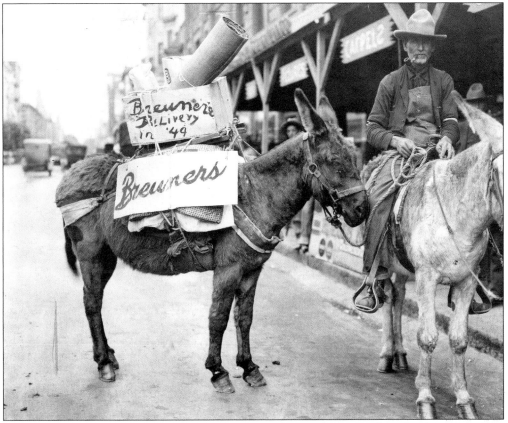

The Days of '49 celebration in 1922 lasted six days and attracted 175,000 visitors. East Sacramento residents and businesses celebrated their connection to Sacramento's founding during the Gold Rush.

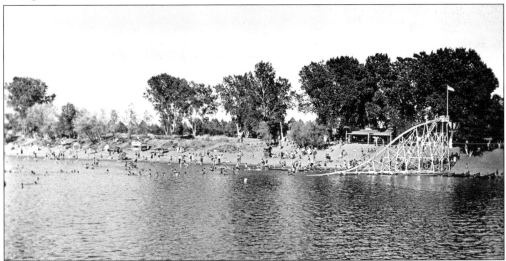

The American River Beach amusement resort, near the H Street bridge, provided East Sacramentans relief from the scorching heat of summer. The resort offered concessions, a waterslide, boating, and dancing, as shown in this 1931 photo.

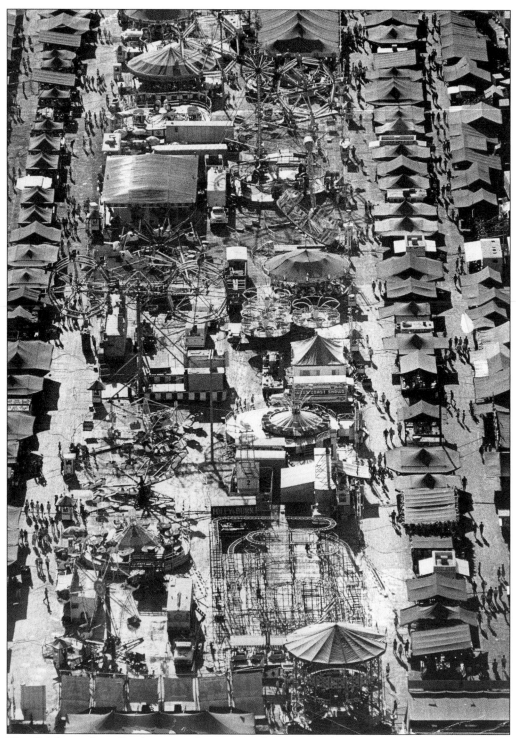

The California State Fair became a Sacramento fixture in 1859. East Sacramentans, along with all Californians, eagerly anticipated this annual event. The fair, shown in this *c.* 1970 photo, remains a popular summer destination.

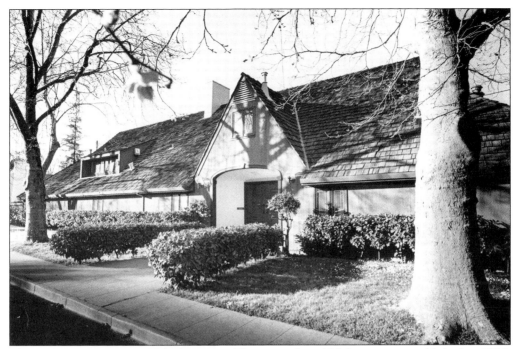

The Sutter Lawn Tennis Club, located at Thirty-ninth and N Street, was established in 1919. An exclusive club with limited membership, many East Sacramentans still find it a privilege to belong to the club, shown in this 1979 photo.

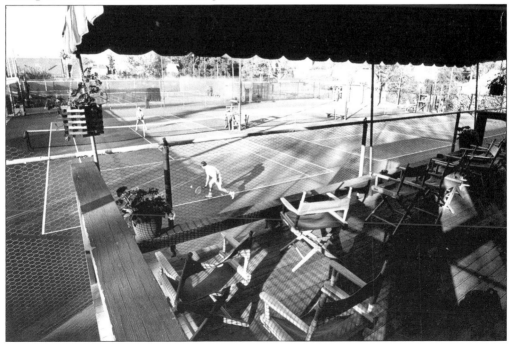

Although the Sutter Lawn tennis courts, shown in this 1979 photo, are currently protected by high fences, longtime East Sacremento residents remember sneaking into the unguarded courts and playing with racquets left behind by members.

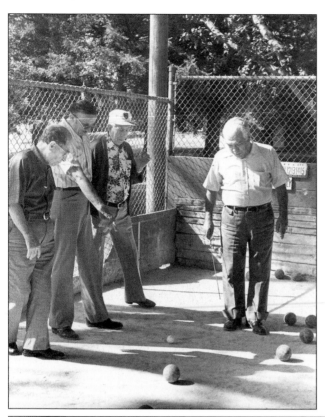

East Portal Park, a reclaimed gravel pit, became the center for bocce ball in East Sacramento. In this 1960 photo, Giussipi Stassi, centered in the background, is the bocce champion.

Members of Turn Verien, a German cultural club established in 1854, participated in many athletic events. The bowling team is pictured here *c.* 1890. Turn Verein's current building is located at Thirty-fourth and J Streets.

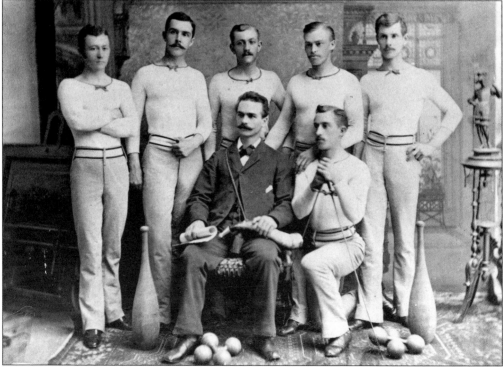

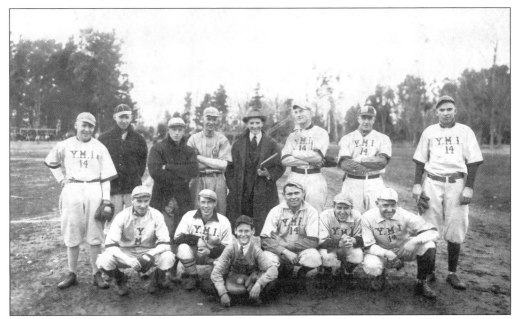

The Young Men's Institute baseball team is photographed here in 1906 in McKinley Park. In the late 1910s, YMI's baseball team, known as the Bushers, was considered the best in the city.

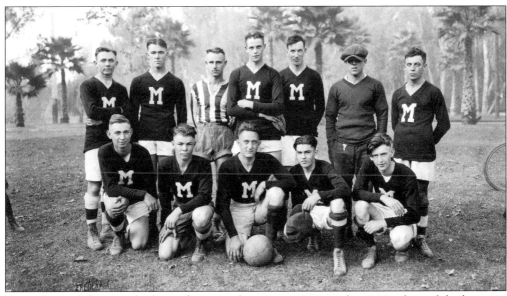

McKinley Park became the home for soccer leagues in 1912. In the 1920s, the park had its own team, the McKinley Parkers, who are featured here. In 1922, the Parkers played the Vampires for the California Cup. The match ended in a tie.

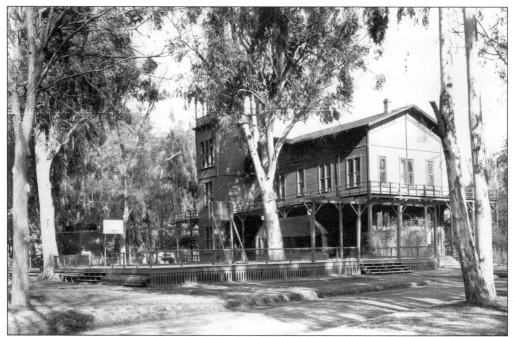

McKinley Park's original clubhouse, shown here c. 1918, had an open-air dance floor that offered space for basketball, dancing, and other community events. This structure was replaced in 1936 by the Florence Turton Clunie Memorial Clubhouse.

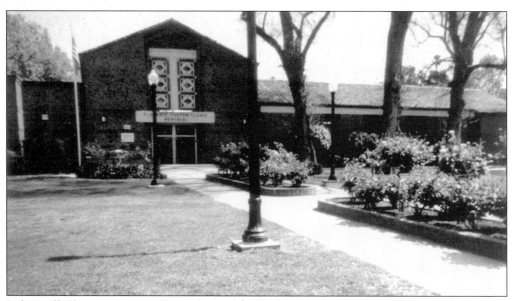

In her will, Florence Turton Clunie donated $150,000 to McKinley Park. This contribution was used to build the current clubhouse, which houses a library, gymnasium, and meeting rooms. (Photo by Audra Hayes, 2004.)

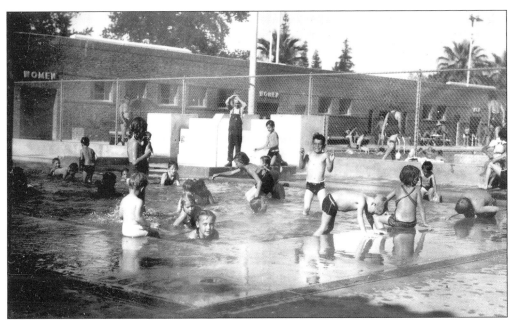

McKinley Park has provided a variety of facilities for children to play, including the wading pool pictured here. In 1993, the small pool was closed due to maintenance expenses.

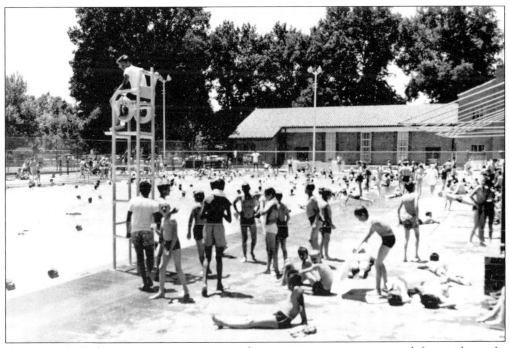

Sacramento's high summer temperatures make aquatic recreation essential for residents. In 1936, East Sacramentans received a neighborhood cooling option with the construction of the Clunie Memorial pool.

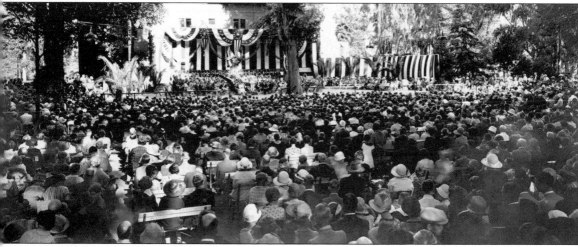

The Sacramento Symphony Orchestra performed on the open-air dance floor of the old McKinley Clubhouse. This performance, c. 1920, was conducted by Franz Dicks, who was the symphony's first conductor.

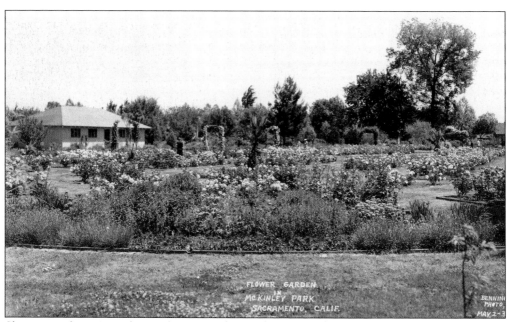

Shown in this 1937 photo, the McKinley Park rose garden is one of the most beautiful attractions in East Sacramento. Developed in 1922, the garden contains more than 150 varieties of roses and covers three-fourths of an acre.

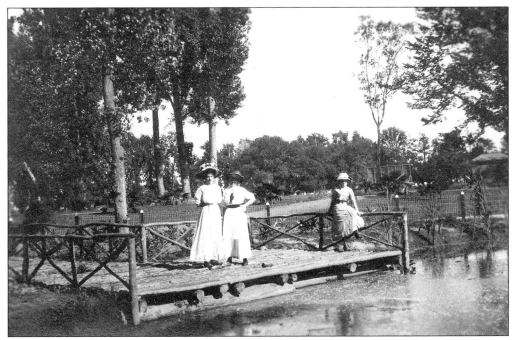

Three women pose beside Lake Kiesel in McKinley Park in 1912. At the time of the park's creation in 1871, the lake was part of Burns's slough. The slough's canals were eventually paved. Lake Kiesel is the only remnant.

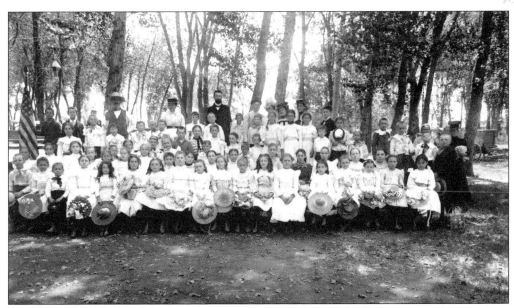

In 1895, Rev. Charles Oehler's German Lutheran Sunday School class enjoyed a picnic in McKinley Park. The church provided the children with food and refreshments. The children also participated in games and races.

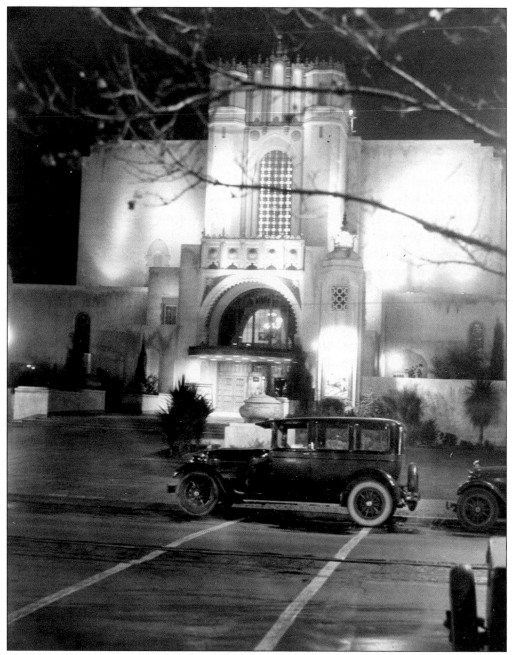

In 1927, the spectacular Alhambra Theater opened on the corner of Thirty-first (renamed Alhambra Boulevard) and J Street. The Moorish theater boasted the first Vitaphone theater sound system in California. The Alhambra was razed in 1973 and a Safeway supermarket was erected on the site.

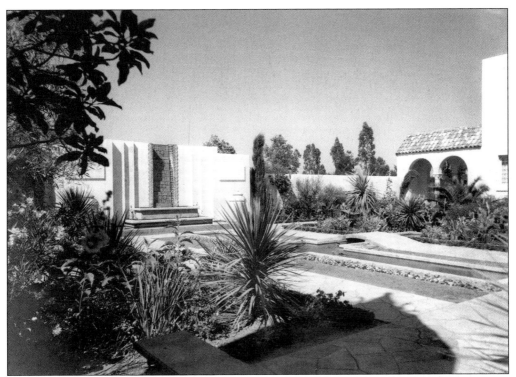

The Alhambra Theater's courtyards drew as much attention as the theater itself. The fountain, shown in this 1929 photo, includes a quote from *The Rubáiyát of Omar Khayyám,* which added to the theater's exotic atmosphere. Safeway retained the fountain, which now can be viewed in the supermarket's parking lot.

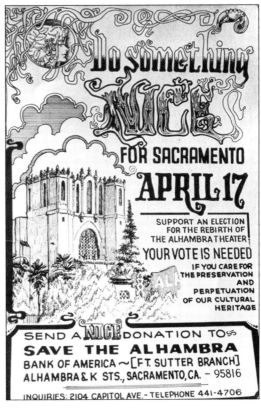

In 1972, local residents rallied support to save the Alhambra Theater from destruction. Activists attempted to raise funds to buy back the theater from Safeway. The preservationists did not receive enough donations. Their next step was to put a $1.5 million bond measure on the ballot. The measure did not pass and the theater was torn down in 1973.

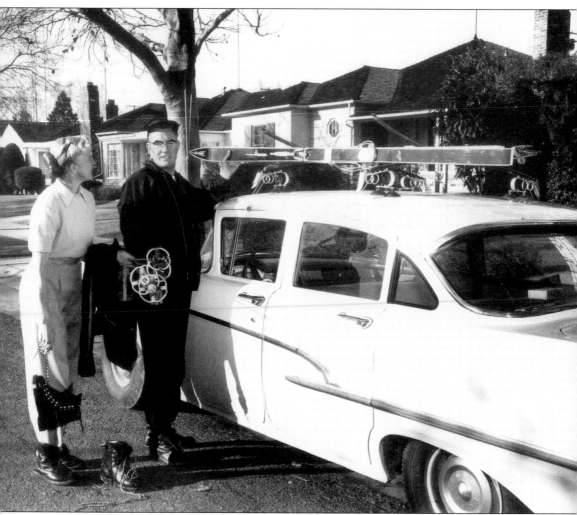

Rose (Mellor) and Mickey Millard prepare to head to Squaw Valley to assist with the 1960 Olympics. Rose was a talented athlete in both summer and winter sports. Her daughter described the Mellor family as bohemian. Family lore contains accounts of snowshoeing into Yosemite instead of driving.

Seven

GETTING THERE
BY DEBBIE POULSEN

At the turn of the 20th century, streetcars, bicycles, horses and buggies, railroads, and automobiles provided transportation for travel to other communities and from the business and entertainment sections of downtown Sacramento to the popular suburb of East Sacramento. This was an exciting era as new methods of travel quickly changed the everyday social, business, shopping, and educational opportunities for all, especially women, youth, and the elderly. No longer was a person dependent on hitching up a horse.

By 1904 there were 27 "horseless carriages" registered in Sacramento County and within ten years, a total of 3,419. By 1914 one of every 20 citizens owned a car. Automobiles brought new freedom for women, especially after the invention of the self-starter. This new freedom was demonstrated on Election Day, October 11, 1911, when one lady suffragette drove her car from precinct to precinct transporting literature and relief workers.

Despite transportation innovations, getting there could still be difficult in the early 20th century. The rainy season and the accompanying mud created a treacherous environment for those on foot. A local bond in 1907 finally provided macadam surfacing for main roads. Traffic traveling east through East Sacramento in 1911 also increased when a bridge was built over the American River at H Street. In 1909 the State Highway Commission was formed, and by 1916, the state had become responsible for maintaining roads.

Transportation was central to the suburban growth experienced in East Sacramento, and change certainly caused the decline of horse and carriage-related businesses. Opportunities unfolded for automobile sightseeing trips, everyday travel, and visits to other communities. The love affair with the automobile rendered streetcars obsolete by the late 1940s.

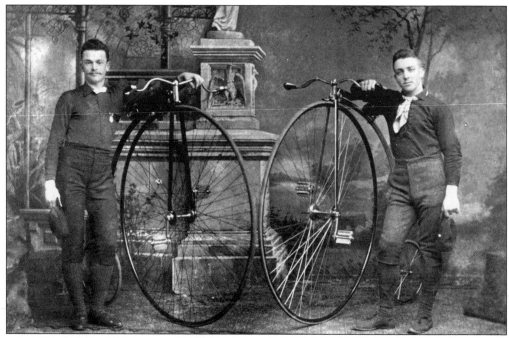

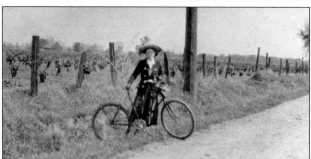

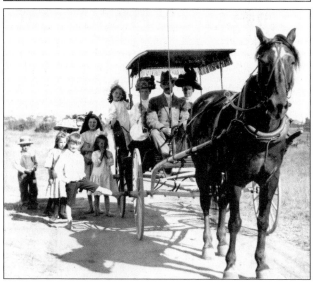

Charles Mier and Louis F. Breuner (above) pose with their bicycles, c. 1890. Mier became the city assessor and Breuner entered the furniture business, started by his German immigrant parents. At this time, the Capitol City Wheelmen, a group of cycling enthusiasts, were responsible for helping the area obtain better roads needed for bicycle excursions.

Ruby Mellor (middle photo) rides her bicycle on H Street in 1922. Old grape vineyards filled much of the countryside at this time.

This horse and buggy (left) driven by Carl Inderkum is typical of those used in the early 1900s. The Inderkum family was involved in the local Golden Eagle Dairy business from 1894 to the 1920s at Fortieth and J Streets. As the automobile became more popular, the need for horses and buggies soon declined.

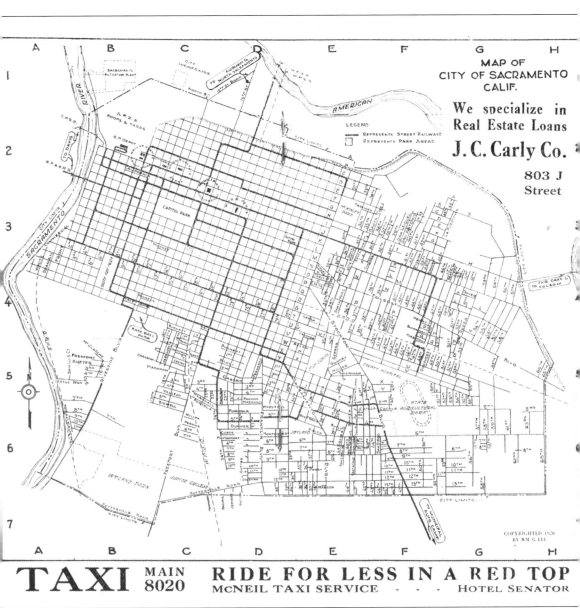

This map of the trolley system for the Sacramento Street Railway was drawn for "Lee's Sacramento Guide," a small booklet published to promote tourism, in July 1926. One line ran north and south on Thirty-first Street, and an eastern line ran on J Street to Forty-sixth Street. It then turned south to R Street, headed east to Forty-eighth Street, and ended within a few blocks.

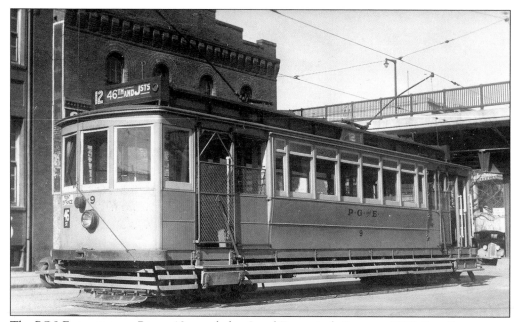

The PG&E streetcar on Route 12 traveled to J and Forty-sixth Street *c.* 1930. East Sacramento residents used this convenient form of transportation to get to downtown Sacramento places of business and entertainment until most families had automobiles in the late 1940s.

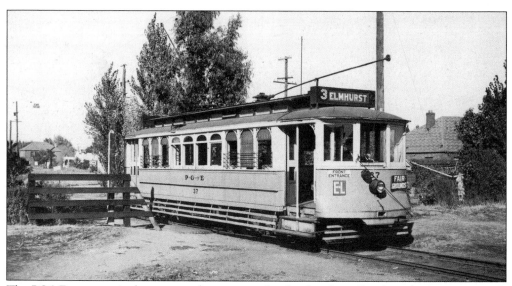

The PG&E streetcar is shown near the cemetery by the Southern Pacific railway crossing at R Street in 1937.

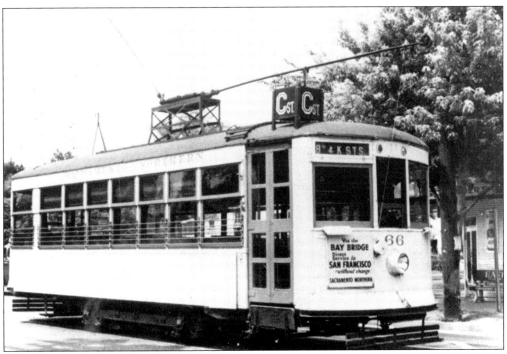

The "End of the Line!" at Alhambra and F Streets, is shown with Solanders Store in the background in the 1940s.

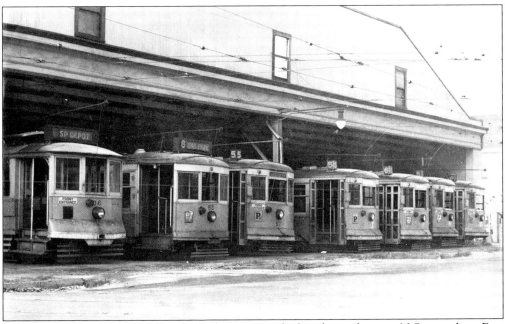

Seven streetcars, shown in this c. 1945 photo, are parked in the car barn on N Street where East Sacramento streetcars spent their off time.

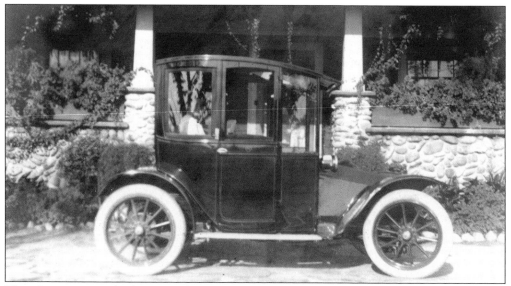

This electric car was built in 1910 by A. Meister and Sons. The Meister family lived on Thirty-ninth Street and operated an iron works factory known regionally for its rail motorcars, rail buses, motorbuses, electric streetcars, and automobile manufacturing.

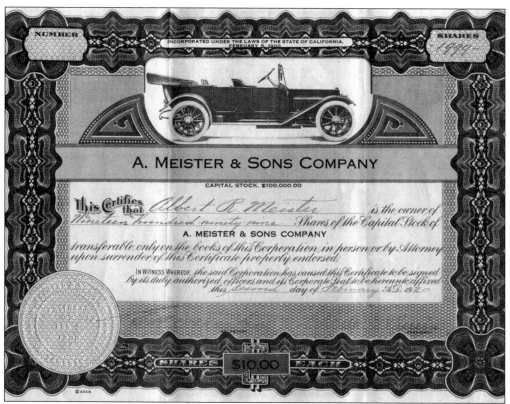

Albert Meister owned nearly 2,000 shares of stock in the A. Meister & Sons Company. This certificate dates from 1920. (Photo courtesy of Marilyn Meister Hanson.)

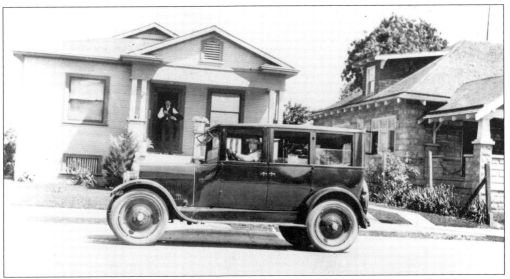

Women enjoyed driving, as shown in this c. 1926 photo of Jennie Lazzarini (age 20). Her father John observes from the porch of their home at Forty-second and F Streets.

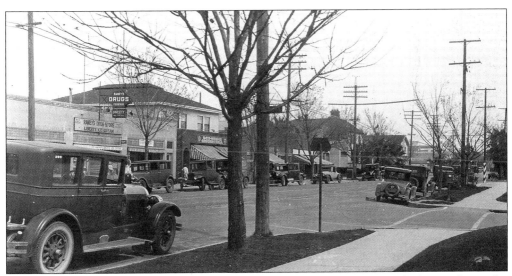

A typical 1929 street scene of J Street looking east from Thirty-seventh Street shows the streetcar line running in the middle of the street. Bicycles and automobiles could drive along on each side.

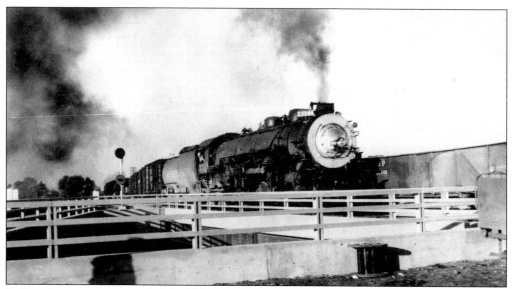

In East Sacramento a train belched black smoke as it passed by the American Can Company at Elvas and C Streets *c.* 1942. Railroad lines ran east and west along the levee on the north and south between R and S Streets.

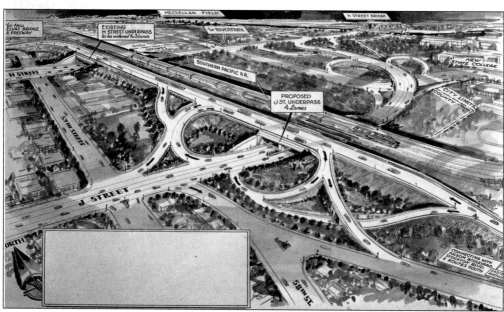

An original sketch map, dated January 27, 1953, lays out plans for the Elvas Street underpass.

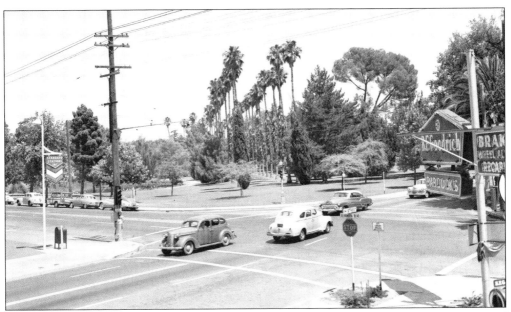

Note the limited traffic controls at the entrance to McKinley Park near the intersection of Alhambra Boulevard and H Street, pictured in the 1950s. Today the intersection has both a light and a traffic control island.

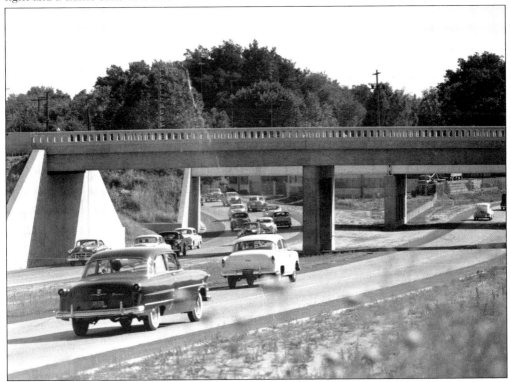

Pictured c. 1950, Elvas Avenue was built as an expressway to bypass the neighborhoods on H Street for travel between Fifty-sixth Street and McKinley Park. It has been deemed by some as the first freeway in Sacramento.

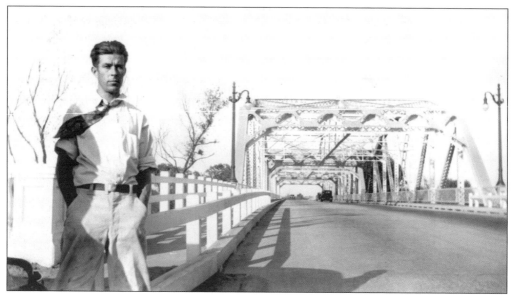

The newly constructed H Street Bridge is admired by Charles Haslam in this *c.* 1933 photo.

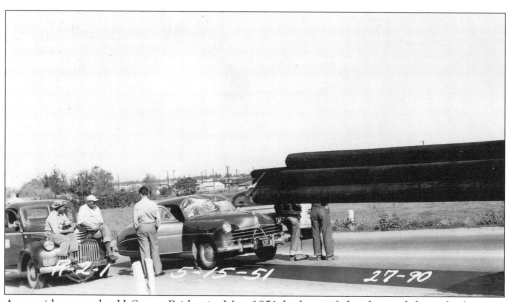

An accident on the H Street Bridge in May 1951 looks as if the driver did not brake soon enough for the unusual load driving in front of him. The onlookers sitting on the hood of the car seem to indicate that no one was seriously injured.

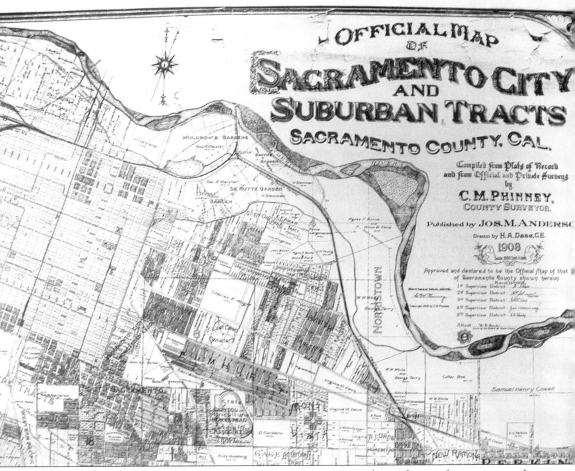

This 1911 map of East Sacramento shows transportation routes limited to surface streets and rail lines.

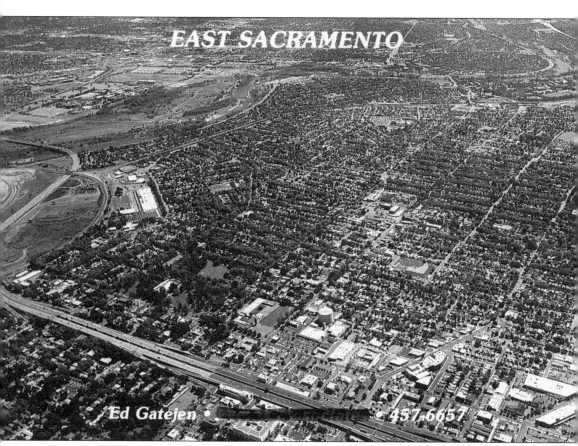

An aerial view of East Sacramento shows transportation byways in the 1960s. This real-estate advertising postcard provides evidence of the transformation of East Sacramento from farm to freeway.

Eight

FAITH AND ETERNAL LIFE
BY RENEE CARTER

Over the last century, churches and parishioners have played a significant role in the stability and longevity of East Sacramento. Today there are approximately ten traditional churches in the community. Two of the congregations, First Christian Church and Faith United Methodist, date back more than 100 years.

In addition to regular church services, local churches provide fundamental support and services for the larger Sacramento community. The Sacred Heart of Jesus and St. Mary's continue to ensure the future of today's youth through small catholic schools. Other congregations, including Faith United Methodist and the Sutter ward of the Church of Jesus Christ of Latter-Day Saints, are extensively involved in outreach programs. Parishioners of the Sutter ward frequently volunteer time and money to support Deseret Industries and a church cannery. The congregation of Faith United Methodist regularly supports local food pantries, Sacramento Valley Teen Challenge, and Project Linus that provide for basic and spiritual needs of the community.

Although East Lawn Memorial Park is the only remaining cemetery in East Sacramento, the community was home to two Gold Rush–era cemeteries. Sutter's New Helvetia Cemetery served as a resting place for many men lured to California by the promise of gold. The Hebrew Benevolent Society established the first Jewish Cemetery in California in 1850. Although both cemeteries are arguably significant to California history, they were both destroyed in the early 20th century. Graves were removed and relocated to the Home of Peace Cemetery, East Lawn Memorial Park, and the City Cemetery.

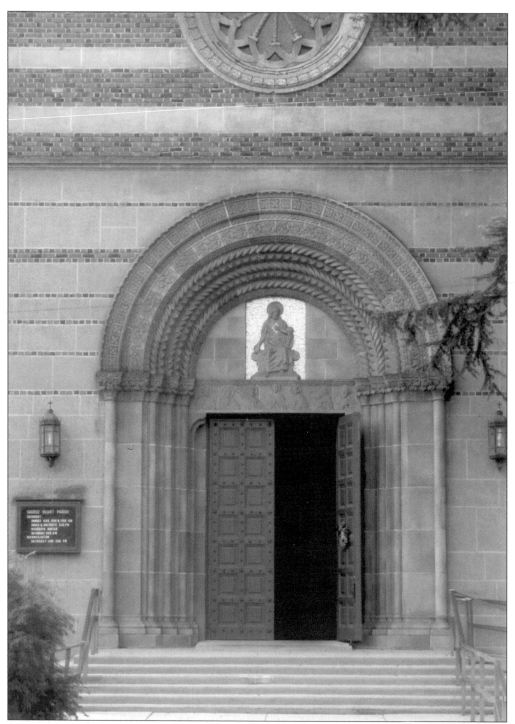

The open doors of the Sacred Heart of Jesus church greet parishioners and citizens of the community. The Roman basilica entry, constructed in 1931, welcomes onlookers and worshippers alike. Note the intricate carving of the Sacred Heart of Jesus over the front door in this *c.* 2000 photo. (Photo courtesy Sacred Heart of Jesus Church.)

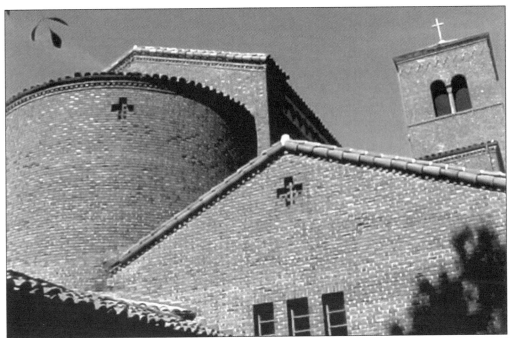

Shown in this *c.* 2000 photo, the exterior of Sacred Heart of Jesus church is constructed out of stained concrete and red brick. The Italian Lombard–style building possesses a belfry, and the bells toll hourly during the day. (Photo courtesy Sacred Heart of Jesus Church.)

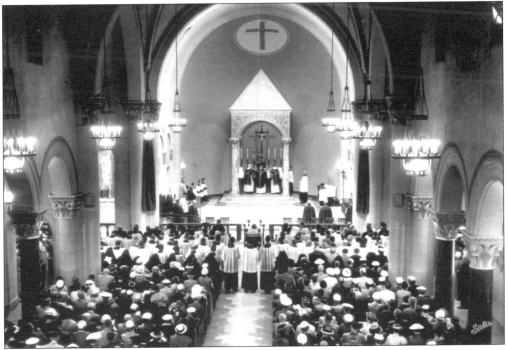

Parishioners grieve over the death of Monsignor Lyons, the second pastor of the Sacred Heart of Jesus Church. Observe the Corinthian columns and ornate images as well as the Romanesque archways throughout the sanctuary. (Photo courtesy Sacred Heart of Jesus Church.)

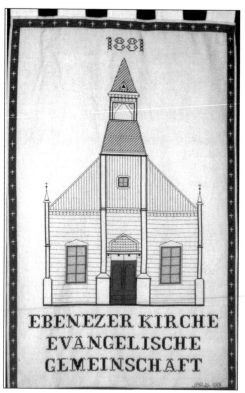

EBENEZER KIRCHE
EVANGELISCHE
GEMEINSCHAFT

This banner, displayed in the sanctuary of Faith United Methodist Church, commemorates the founding of the church in 1881. The hand-stitched banner venerates the original building. Observe the German text at the bottom of the banner, which notes the central ethnicity of founding members. The church moved to its present location on Thirty-sixth and J Streets in 1964. (Photo by Renee Carter, 2004.)

In 1948, St. Mary's Church relocated to its present location in East Sacramento. The new building provided much needed space for the growing congregation. In addition to the church, this site now houses a parochial school, parish hall, and gymnasium.

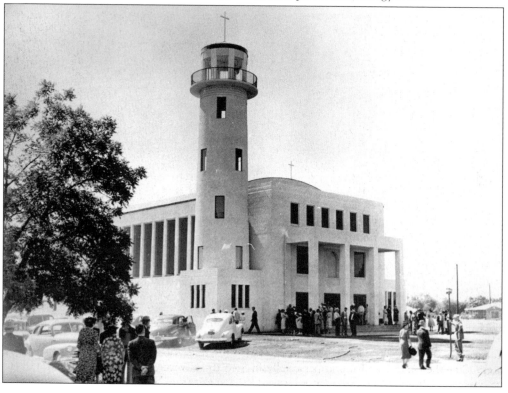

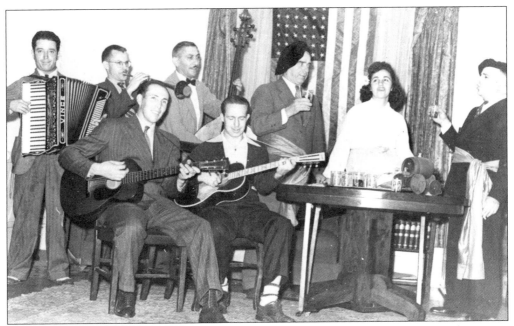

Parishioners of St. Mary's Church often gathered together outside of the church. This young group performed an Italian song and dance for friends in 1947.

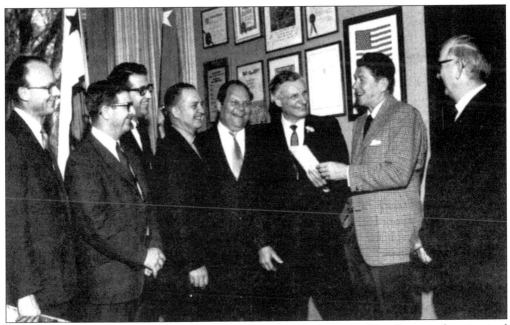

Missionary delegates of the Church of Jesus Christ of Latter Day Saints often invited community and state leaders to visit the church. This delegation visited Gov. Ronald Reagan c. 1970 at the State Capitol and personally invited the governor to visit the church. (Photo courtesy the Church of Jesus Christ of Latter-Day Saints, Sutter Ward.)

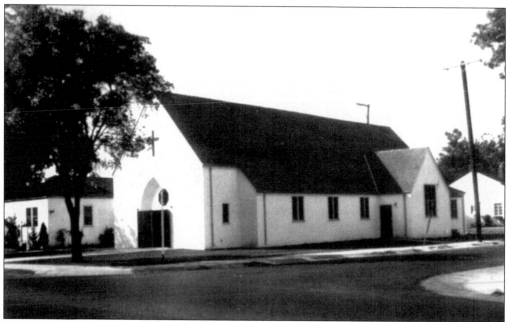

Shown in this *c.* 1950 photo, Lutheran Church of the Cross possesses a small but loyal congregation. (Photo courtesy John Ranlett.)

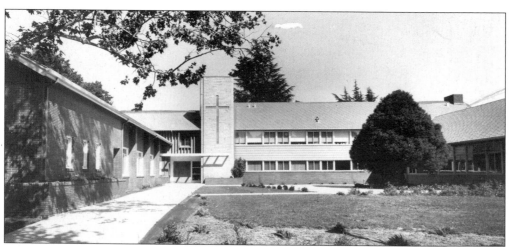

Rev. Peter R. Burnett renamed the congregation Disciples of Christ to the First Christian Church after he announced, "You are the Disciples and are called Christians first at Sacramento." This undated photo shows the interior courtyard of the First Christian Church at its present location at Folsom Boulevard and Thirty-ninth Street.

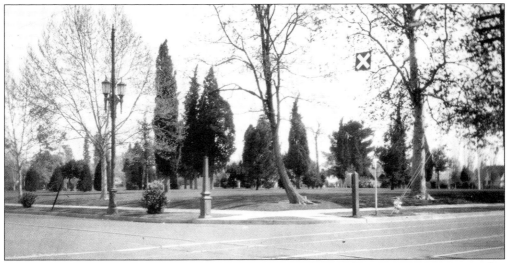

New Helvetia Cemetery was in pristine condition in early March 1936. However, soon after this photo was taken, the city of Sacramento removed more than 5,230 graves and demolished the cemetery to build a freeway and junior high school. The graves, including Sacramento's first mayor Hardin Bigelow, were relocated to East Lawn Cemetery and the city cemetery.

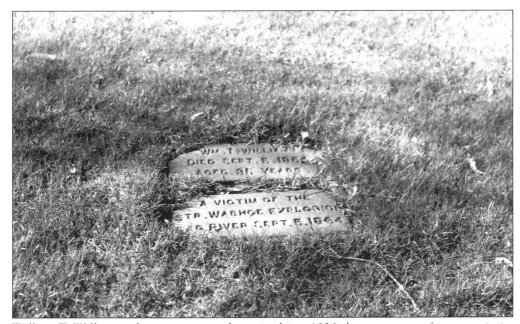

William T. Williams, whose gravesite is shown in this c. 1936 photo, was an unfortunate victim of the horrible Steamer *Washoe* explosion on September 5, 1864. The deceased was laid to rest in New Helvetia Cemetery. More than 90 people perished when the boilers exploded on the Sacramento River.

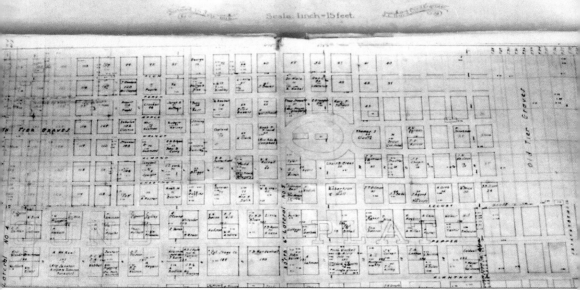

John Sutter established New Helvetia Cemetery during the California gold rush. The cemetery housed the remains of cholera victims, Chinese miners, and those killed during the Squatter Riots of 1850. This original plat map illustrates the location and size of grave plots throughout the cemetery.

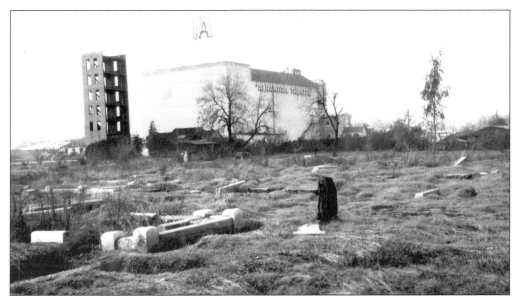

The first Jewish cemetery in California was originally located in East Sacramento at Thirty-second and J Streets. Although the graves had already been removed and transferred to a new cemetery, the remnants of the cemetery were still present in March 1936. Observe the Alhambra Theater in the background.

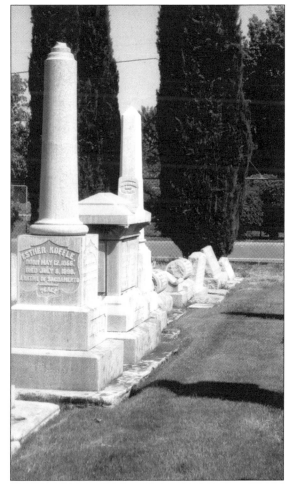

In 1924 the Jewish cemetery was moved to its present location at 6200 Stockton Boulevard. Entire graves at the original cemetery were transferred and interred at the new Home of Peace Cemetery. (Photo by Renee Carter, 2000.)

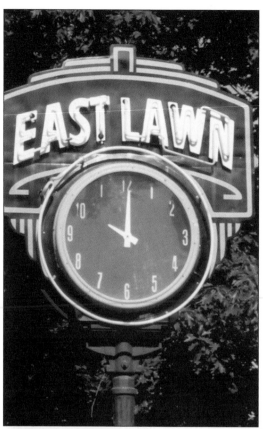

For more than 100 years, East Lawn Cemetery and Memorial Park have been part of the community of East Sacramento. The East Lawn clock welcomes visitors. (Photo by Renee Carter, 2004.)

The Memorial Park is tastefully landscaped in order to ensure a calm and quiet atmosphere. (Photo by Renee Carter, 2004.)

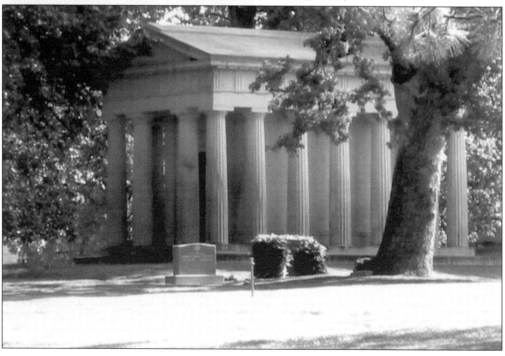

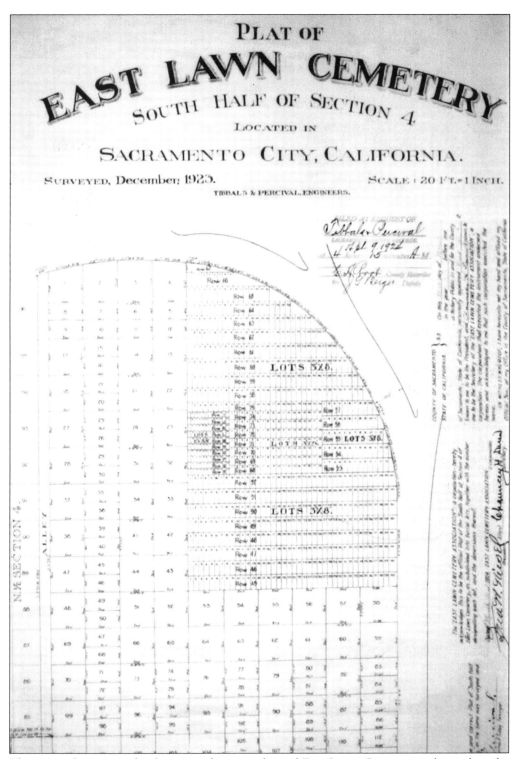

The original 1923 south plat map of section four of East Lawn Cemetery is located at the Sacramento Archives and Museum Collection Center. Observe the discrepancy in plot sizes.

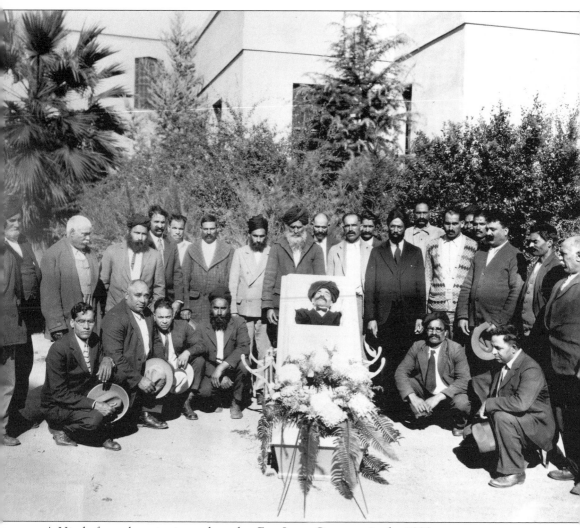

A Hindu funeral service is conducted at East Lawn Cemetery in the 1930s.

Nine

EMERGENCY

BY RENEE CARTER

At the time of annexation, East Sacramento did not possess its own city services. The community relied upon the city of Sacramento to provide essential services, including hospitals, fire stations, and police protection. However, soon after annexation, these essential services proved integral to the growing community. Hospitals and fire stations soon appeared in East Sacramento.

The city of Sacramento founded the police and fire departments shortly after adopting its first city charter in 1850. At that time, the fledgling city possessed a volunteer fire department and a single sheriff. Today the police and fire departments employ more than 1,200 men and women throughout the city. More importantly, the citizens of East Sacramento recognize the vital contributions made by the police and fire departments. Recently, community members united in order to preserve a key landmark, Chemical Fire Station No. 4, associated with the history of the fire department in East Sacramento.

The community is also home to two state-of-the-art medical centers. Both hospitals, Mercy General and Sutter Memorial, are regarded as models for other hospitals throughout the nation. Since its relocation to East Sacramento in 1925, Mercy General has become a leader in stroke research. Sutter Memorial, part of Sutter Medical Center and founded in the early 1920s, is considered the "area's most comprehensive health care provider." Together, the hospitals employ more than 1,000 physicians, nurses, and other support staff.

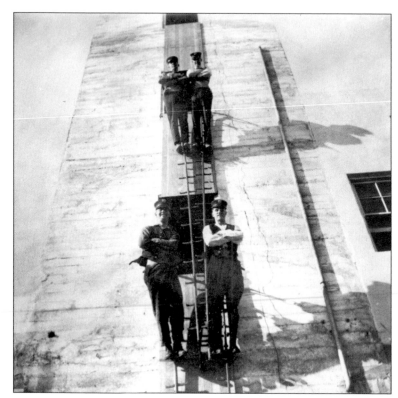

This undated photo was taken at the firefighter-training facility near Alhambra Boulevard. It is significant to note the dress of the firefighters, particularly the hats, and the type of ladder on which they are standing. The ladder has a central handle; modern-day ladders possess handles on both sides.

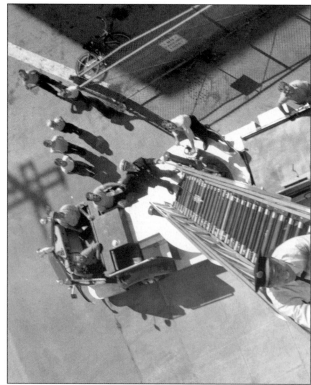

This 1966 bird's-eye view was probably taken from the top of the firehouse and showcases the fire department's new ladder truck.

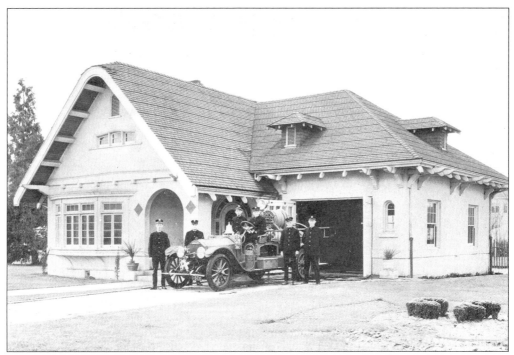

Shown in this *c.* 1920 photo is the first East Sacramento Fire Station, Chemical Station No. 4, which opened in East Sacramento in 1916. Originally located at 3721 M Street, the station relocated to 3720 Folsom Boulevard in 1917.

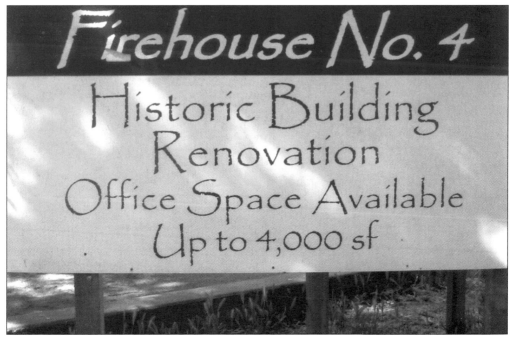

Although Chemical Station No. 4 was abandoned and fell into disrepair, local citizens rallied community leaders, and the station is now undergoing restoration. The rehabilitated building will be used as office space. (Photo by Renee Carter, 2004.)

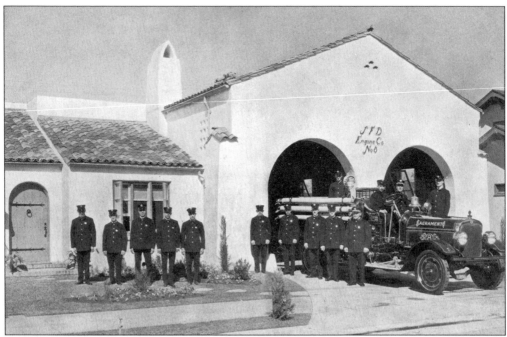

By 1925, East Sacramento possessed a second fire station Engine Company No. 8, located at 5990 H Street.

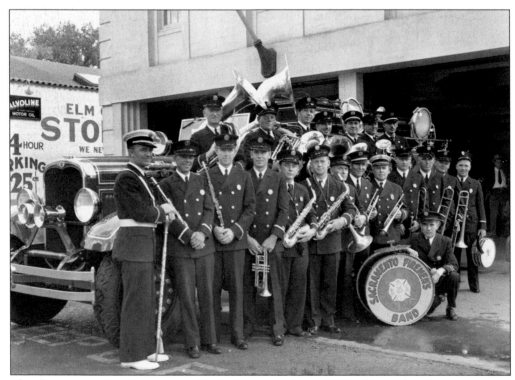

The Sacramento Fire Department Band, shown in this c. 1930 photo, played at community events throughout the city of Sacramento.

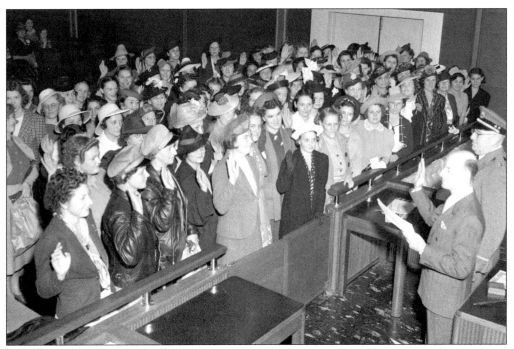

In 1939, the Sacramento Police Department hired women as traffic patrol officers. This induction ceremony included more than 50 women of various ages.

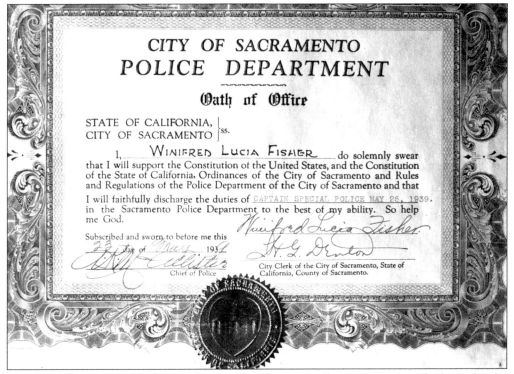

CITY OF SACRAMENTO
POLICE DEPARTMENT

Oath of Office

STATE OF CALIFORNIA, } ss.
CITY OF SACRAMENTO

I, WINIFRED LUCIA FISHER do solemnly swear that I will support the Constitution of the United States, and the Constitution of the State of California, Ordinances of the City of Sacramento and Rules and Regulations of the Police Department of the City of Sacramento and that

I will faithfully discharge the duties of CAPTAIN SPECIAL POLICE MAY 25, 1939. in the Sacramento Police Department to the best of my ability. So help me God.

Subscribed and sworn to before me this 23 day of May, 193_

_____
Chief of Police

Winifred Lucia Fisher

H. G. Denton
City Clerk of the City of Sacramento, State of California, County of Sacramento.

In order to become full-fledged traffic patrol and special officers, the women had to take the oath of office of the Sacramento Police Department.

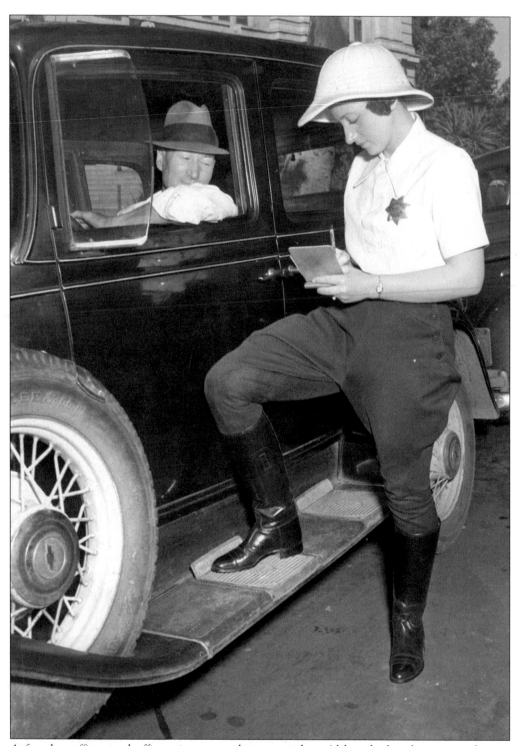

A female traffic patrol officer gives a gentleman a ticket. Although the photo was taken in 1939, this female officer is wearing long pants.

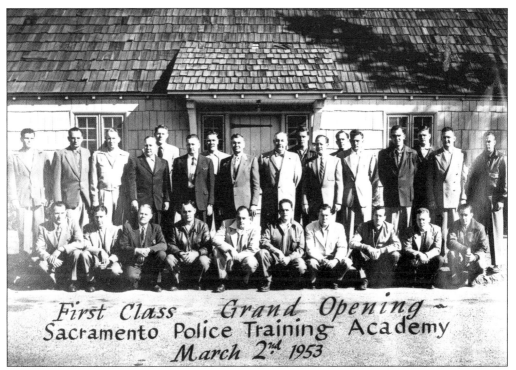

First Class — Grand Opening —
Sacramento Police Training Academy
March 2nd 1953

The Sacramento Police Training Academy opened on March 2, 1953, in McKinley Park. The Sacramento Police Department used the Clunie clubhouse as a school to educate and train police officers. James V. Hicks, the captain of the department, is present in this photo.

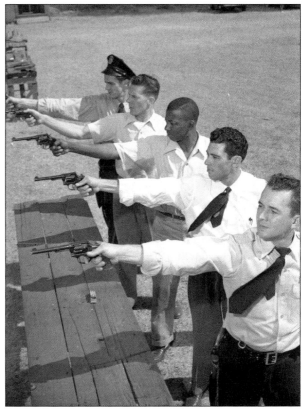

Police officers and cadets practice shooting their guns at an unknown location. Although the exact date of the photo is also unknown, it is possible it was taken at the Sacramento Police Training Academy at McKinley Park. The cars are characteristic of the 1950s. However, if the date of the photo is during that time period, it is worth noting the presence of an African-American cadet in the photo.

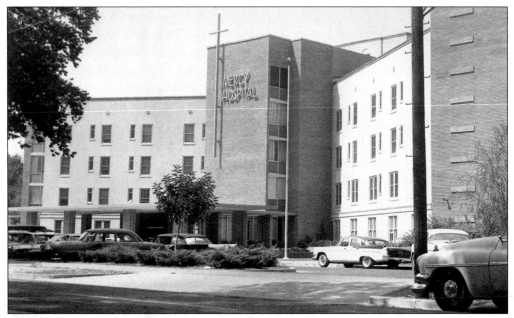

Mater Misericordae Hospital, now renamed Mercy General Hospital, relocated to its present location in the early 1930s. The Sisters of Mercy spent more than a decade raising funds for the new hospital. This photo, taken in 1959, shows the exterior of the hospital.

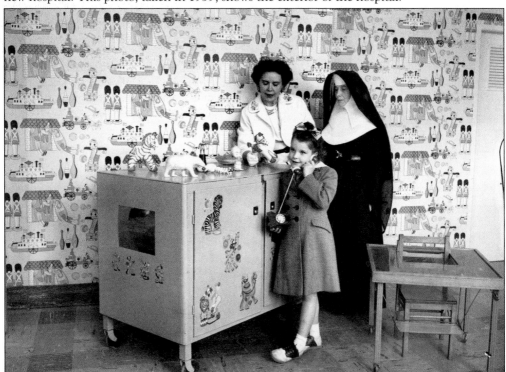

The Sisters of Mercy took a "hands-on" approach with their patients. They frequently visited children and families in the hospital. This 1953 photo highlights the new children's addition to the hospital.

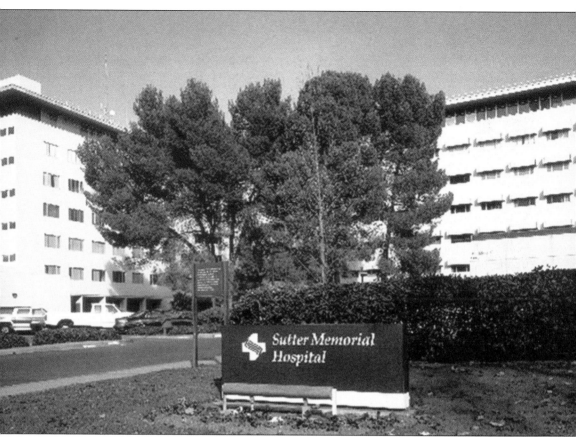

Local physicians established Sutter Memorial hospital after a rampant influenza epidemic in the early 1920s. Today Sutter Memorial is one of the premiere regional hospitals providing new procedures and state-of-the-art technology. (Photo courtesy Rosemary Navarro, Sutter Health.)

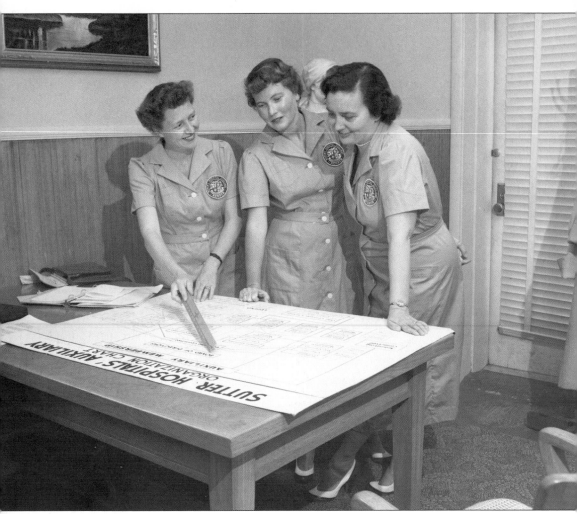

The Sutter Hospitals' Auxiliary is a "service organization" comprised of community volunteers. The auxiliary raises money through gift shop sales. This 1950s photo shows auxiliary volunteers reviewing an organizational chart.